THE
BEACHES
OF WALES

THE BEACHES OF WALES

A COMPLETE GUIDE TO EVERY BEACH AND COVE AROUND THE WELSH COASTLINE

First published in 2020 by Vertebrate Publishing.

VERTEBRATE PUBLISHING
Omega Court, 352 Cemetery Road, Sheffield S11 8FT, United Kingdom.
www.v-publishing.co.uk

A CIP catalogue record for this book is available from the British Library.

ISBN 978-1-912560-93-6 (Paperback)
ISBN 978-1-912560-94-3 (Ebook)

Front cover: Whiteford Sands, Swansea.
Back cover: L–R: Pembrey Beach, Pembrokeshire; Porth yr Halen, Llanddwyn Island; Coastal Path at Telpyn,
Carmarthenshire; Traeth-yr-ynys, Ceredigion; Causeway to Sandy Bay looking out towards St Margaret's Island,
Bullum's Bay, Caldey Island; Sea pink; Porth yr Ogof, Llanddwyn Island; Three Cliffs Bay, The Gower Peninsula.
Photos of Cribach Bay © QinetiQ, Aberporth.
Photos of Bodorgan © Off The Ground Aerial Imaging.
All other photography by Alistair Hare.

Design by Jane Beagley, production by Rosie Edwards, Vertebrate Publishing.

Printed and bound in Europe by Latitude Press.

Vertebrate Publishing is committed to printing on paper from sustainable sources.

Acknowledgements
I would like to express my thanks to QinetiQ, Aberporth for supplying the images
of Cribach Bay. Also to the staff at MoD Castlemartin Range for allowing me access
to their beaches. Finally, to the staff at Fishguard Port for allowing me to photograph Pwll Hir.

THE
BEACHES
OF WALES

A COMPLETE GUIDE TO EVERY BEACH
AND COVE AROUND THE WELSH COASTLINE

ALISTAIR HARE

Vertebrate Publishing, Sheffield
www.v-publishing.co.uk

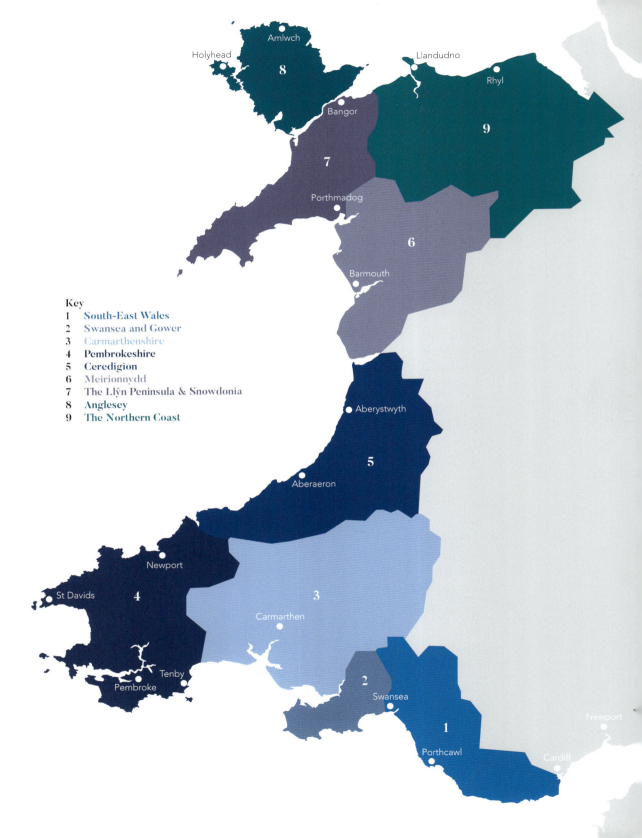

Key
1 **South-East Wales**
2 **Swansea and Gower**
3 Carmarthenshire
4 **Pembrokeshire**
5 **Ceredigion**
6 Meirionnydd
7 The Llŷn Peninsula & Snowdonia
8 **Anglesey**
9 **The Northern Coast**

Opposite Porth Tywyn Mawr, Anglesey

Introduction

Surrounded on three sides by water, Wales has hundreds of beaches to choose from. Although many guides are available, few describe the beaches in enough detail to give a clear impression of what to expect. Even fewer list small, remote coves, and surprisingly no guide has included every beach and cove around the coast of Wales – until now.

Many visitors will return to the same beaches, either because they don't know about other places or don't want to risk travelling to somewhere new to find it's not what was expected. For this book I have photographed the beaches of Wales on sunny days, usually with a low tide and from the best viewpoint I could find. Accompanying these are descriptions covering aspects such as parking, dog restrictions, access, any hazards, and facilities. The beaches are listed in clockwise order around the coast. Where more than one beach is listed under one heading clockwise order has been kept.

How many beaches are there in Wales?

To answer this, a clear definition is needed as to what constitutes a beach. For the purposes of this book, I have included every beach which has a name, provided it's not so small or muddy as to be of little interest. The total is approximately 500. To avoid making long tables of beaches and their facilities I have highlighted this information in symbols found in each entry:

P Parking (within easy walking distance of the beach)

≋ Railway station

☕ Food and drink

⊛ Lifeguarded

WC Toilets

☺ Dogs allowed*

☺ Dog restriction or access for dogs difficult – see text for more information*

☺ Dogs banned*

! Access may be difficult – see text for more information

*Dog information is provided where there is explicit or known access or restrictions. Smaller coves and little-visited beaches often do not have clear access information. Please adhere to any local signage when visiting beaches or coves with your dog.

Where a beach is known by more than one name, or by both English and Welsh names, I have used its most commonly used name. The map references given are usually at the main point of access to the beach.

Access and ownership

Generally, the area of the shore between the mean high and low tide marks is owned by the Crown, managed by local authorities and freely accessible to all. Some beaches in other ownership include Margam Sands in South Wales, owned by Tata Steel, and Pembrey Beach in Carmarthenshire, owned by Carmarthenshire Council. However, for some beaches, particularly in north-west Wales, the land above the high water mark and sometimes part of the foreshore is the property of local landowners. Although there currently appear to be no access restrictions, this may change. Attempts to prevent public access are usually met by fierce local opposition, but any reference in this book to 'access' does not imply a public right of access or right of way.

Disclaimer

This book is offered to provide useful information on the beaches of Wales and is not a recommendation to visit them. It must be remembered that no beach can be considered to be completely safe and getting to some beaches can be dangerous. The use of the information contained herein is therefore entirely at your own risk. Every effort has been made to ensure that the information in this book is correct, but no warranty, express or implied, is given about the plenitude, accuracy or reliability of the information contained herein. Any reliance you place on such information is strictly at your own risk. In no event will the author or publisher be liable for any loss or damage including without limitation, indirect or consequential loss or damage whatsoever arising from the use of this book.

Beach Safety

Find out about the beach and tide times before you enter the sea
Ask the lifeguards or observe local signage.

Take care with inflatables
Check the wind speed and direction before using inflatables in the sea. Never use them in heavy surf, or in strong or offshore winds. On lifeguarded beaches, an orange windsock will be flown if winds are blowing offshore.

Don't sit under cliffs
Always keep a safe distance in case of rockfall.

Supervise young children
Don't let them enter the water or wander off by themselves – much of a lifeguard's time is spent searching for lost children.

Swim within your ability
If you're not a strong swimmer or not used to sea swimming, go to a lifeguarded beach. The red and yellow flags indicate the area patrolled by lifeguards: a red flag means conditions are too dangerous for bathing, while a black and white quartered flag marks an area for watersports.

Note that lifeguards have to train regularly – their usual duty times are from 10 a.m. to 6 p.m. If lifeguards are on the beach outside these times, they may be training. Although they will of course respond to any incidents that arise, they will not be actively patrolling the beach and the red and yellow flags will not be displayed.

At the time of writing, most of the main beaches in the southern half of Wales (i.e. south of the River Dyfi) are patrolled by lifeguards during the summer, whereas in the northern half of Wales only Rhyl and Prestatyn provide that service. The counties of Gwynedd and Anglesey do not employ beach lifeguards.

Swim where and when it's safe
Check the sea conditions before entering the sea. Surf may look fun, but there can be rip currents. Lifeguarded beaches are the safest places to swim, and the high tide period is generally the safest time. Deeply indented bays are usually safe, as are long, straight sandy shores away from river estuaries, although there may be a cross-current on these. Steeply sloping sands usually indicate fast currents. Dry depressions and channels in the sand are often caused by rips.

Beware of currents
A rip current is defined as water flowing out to sea. These can be recognised by an area of calmer water in breaking waves, and discoloration caused by sand being picked up off the bottom. Rips and other strong currents can occur:
- » Near points, headlands and harbour walls.
- » Between islands and the mainland.
- » On beaches in the vicinity of a strong tidal flow.
- » Near river estuaries.
- » In surf conditions.

Rips are rarely very wide, and if caught in one, you should:
- » Try to stand, and wade out of it if possible.
- » Stay calm.
- » Raise your hand and shout for help.
- » Swim across rather than against it, and make for the shore when free.

Take care not to get cut off by the tide
Places you're likely to get cut off include:
- » Bays or long stretches of coast backed by high cliffs.
- » Causeways.
- » Sandbars.
- » Wide bays/estuaries with little gradient.

If you venture into such places be sure you know the tide times and which way the tide is going. Large areas of sand may look flat but are usually

1 Monkstone, rip currents **2** Traeth Abermenai, sand with little gradient will flood quickly on a rising tide
3 A red flag indicates conditions are too dangerous for bathing **4** A black and white quartered flag indicates
the area for launching, surfing and other sports; a red and yellow flag indicates the area patrolled by lifeguards

a maze of banks and water channels which quickly fill on the incoming tide.

Don't dig deep or tunnel into sand
Sand is unstable and very heavy. Tunnels will collapse without warning.

Jumping/diving from rocks
Have fun, but take care:

> » Check the water regularly for depth, obstructions and currents – on Bristol Channel coasts the water depth can drop by a foot in ten minutes.
> » Don't do it where you have to jump outwards to avoid an obstruction.
> » Don't jump from heights you're not comfortable with.

Mud
Some beaches along the Bristol Channel, particularly those near to river estuaries (Jersey Marine, Swansea Bay, Llanelli), have thick mud on the lower shore. Should you find yourself sinking, try to go back the way you came. If the mud rises over your shoes, take them off.

On Welsh beaches it is unlikely you will find enough mud to get into serious difficulty, but if you should start sinking deep then spread your weight by crawling or lying down and rolling yourself out. Mud has a high specific gravity so you won't sink under it.

If you see someone in difficulty ...
If there are lifeguards around, tell them; they're the experts who will know what to do. Otherwise:

> » Reaching rescues – if a casualty can be reached with a rope, pole or lifebelt, this is the safest course of action, but bear in mind a panicking swimmer will pull hard on any rope, so be sure you can't get pulled into deep water yourself.
> » Deep water swimming rescues – stop first and assess the situation, and if possible get someone to phone the coastguard. Deep water rescues are risky, but as a general rule they should only be attempted if you are suitably trained AND have an item of rescue equipment available (such as a rescue board). You should not approach within four metres of a casualty unless you have something unsinkable between you, or you have passed a rescue aid and the casualty is calm.
> » Look around – can anyone else help? Surfers, kayakers or scuba divers are usually confident in most water conditions and may be able to assist.
> » Phone the coastguard – call 999 or 112 and ask for the coastguard.

Wildlife Hazards

Jellyfish

Fortunately in Wales most jellyfish are relatively harmless and stings can be easily treated. The sting is caused by specialised cells called nematocysts, which are triggered by contact and inject venom into the victim. If stung the current advice is to rinse with seawater (not fresh water) then remove any stinging cells with tweezers or scrape with a straight edge, such as a bank card. Soak the affected area in water as hot as the casualty can stand for about twenty minutes. Soaked towels can be used if necessary.

Moon jellyfish are the most common, have a mild sting and can be identified by the four pink or purple gonad rings in the bell. Barrel jellyfish can be up to a metre wide and are sometimes washed ashore in their thousands, but only have a very mild sting.

Compass, Lion's Mane and Blue jellyfish are stinging species, more often seen in North Wales than South. Compass jellyfish are up to thirty centimetres wide and can be recognised by the brown Y-shaped markings. Lion's Mane are twenty to fifty centimetres wide, and recognisable by their rust-brown colour. Blue jellyfish are smaller and easily identified by their dark purple colour.

Portuguese Man-of-war are not true jellyfish but siphonophores: colonies of individual organisms dependent upon each other. Rarely seen in Wales, they inflict a serious sting. Closely related are the harmless By-the-wind Sailors, which have a triangular sail.

5 Portuguese Man-of-war **6** Blue jellyfish **7** By-the-wind Sailor **8** **Mewslade, Gower,** adder on the Coast Path

Weever fish

Weever fish are ten to fifteen centimetres long and bury themselves just under the sand at low tide. The poison in their painful sting is neutralised by immersing the affected part in hot water (as hot as the casualty can stand). Lifeguards or first aid facilities should be able to provide this.

Adders

Adders can often be seen on dunes and coastal paths. They are Britain's only venomous snake and are easily identified by a zigzag stripe along their back. This camouflages them well against a stony background. Away from the beach,

wear proper shoes, never put your hand into rock crevices and be careful if walking through heather.

There are about a hundred incidents of adder bites per year in Britain, and in the very unlikely event of being bitten, you need to get to A&E as quickly as possible – by ambulance if necessary. Also remove any bracelets or watches which could cause problems when the affected part swells up. The only other snake you're likely to see is the harmless grass snake, which has distinctive yellow markings behind its head.

The first seaside town in the south-east corner of Wales is Penarth in the Vale of Glamorgan. Being close to major river estuaries, the seawater in this part of Wales is usually a muddy brown colour, slowly becoming clearer as we head west. The shores consist mostly of sandstone rocks and pebbles until Barry Island, which has three sandy bays. Beyond Barry the beaches become rocky again, backed by high unstable cliffs of Blue Lias.

Inland, the Vale is relatively flat with good roads and footpaths, making it a good choice for cycling and walking. A few castles and ancient monuments dot the landscape, including cromlechs at St Lythans and Tinkinswood.

West of the Ogmore river are the counties of Bridgend and Port Talbot. With a relatively flat coastal zone, the beaches are long and sandy, backed mostly by low dunes.

SOUTH-EAST WALES

Opposite Temple Bay, the view east

Penarth

GRID REF **ST 190713**
GPS **51.4344°N, 3.1654°W**
COUNTY **Vale of Glamorgan**
BEACH FACES **East**

Located three miles south of Cardiff, Penarth has a beach of pebbles and low-tide sand, backed by a promenade. It looks out towards the lighthouse of Monkstone Rock in the Bristol Channel and Clevedon on the opposite side. The islands of Steep Holm and Flat Holm are to the south. Being close to river estuaries, the seawater is usually a muddy brown colour and there are strong currents. North of the beach, you'll find one of the best sites in Wales for fossil collecting; ammonites and gryphaea are often found on the high cliffs. As this is a Site of Special Scientific Interest (SSSI), extracting fossils from the living rock is not permitted.

Roadside parking is available on the one-way Esplanade and on the hill to the south, and beach access is down steps or a slipway. Facilities include restaurants, takeaways, toilets and a pier. Penarth Railway Station and town centre are a fifteen-minute walk away through the park of Alexandra Gardens. A dog ban operates from May to September inclusive.

Ranny Bay & Lavernock Point

Ranny Bay

GRID REF **ST 187683**
GFS **51.4074°N, 3.1690°W**
COUNTY **Vale of Glamorgan**
BEACH FACES **South-east**

South of Penarth, the next access point to the shore is from Fort Road (a no through road from the B4267). This leads past St Lawrence's church, ending near the coastal path where some parking space is available. From the coastal path, a short rough path leads on to the pebbly shore.

To the north is Ranny Bay, a beach of pebbles backed by cliffs of sandstone and mudstone, with a lower shore of mud and seaweed. A shingle spit juts out into the channel, and is popular with anglers.

Lavernock Point lies to the south, and is a beach of sand, rocks and shingle backed by high cliffs. Tide permitting, it can be reached by walking around the point, or by walking back from St Mary's Well Bay. A popular beach for fossil collecting, ammonites and ichthyosaur bones are often found. A previously unknown dinosaur, the dracoraptor, was discovered here in 2015. The area is an SSSI, and so extracting fossils from the living rock is not permitted.

St Mary's Well Bay

GRID REF **ST 175675**
GPS **51.4000°N, 3.1861°W**
COUNTY **Vale of Glamorgan**
BEACH FACES **South-east**

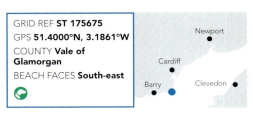

Backed by low cliffs and a holiday park, St Mary's Well Bay is a beach of sandstone and mudstone pebbles, with a lower shore of sand and rocks. Roadside parking is available on Fort Road (a no through road off the B4267) just before the entrance to Marconi Holiday Park. The coastal path leaves the road here, passing through Lavernock Point Nature Reserve. Overlooking the bay is the ruin of Lavernock Fort, beyond which is a short, steep path on to the shore.

Swanbridge

GRID REF **ST 166674**
GPS **51.3990°N, 3.1990°W**
COUNTY **Vale of Glamorgan**
BEACH FACES **South**

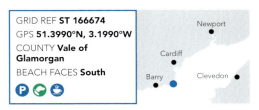

At Swanbridge, the appropriately named Beach Road leads from the B4267 to a beach of rocks and sand. Overlooking the beach is a car park and a seafront pub. Sully Island lies about 400 metres offshore and can be reached via a causeway for approximately three hours either side of low tide. Signs warn that crossing can be dangerous and there have been drownings. If you make the trip across, be sure you know the tide times and allow ample time for your return.

Sully Bay

GRID REF **ST 152678**
GPS **51.4023°N, 3.2192°W**
COUNTY **Vale of Glamorgan**
BEACH FACES **South**

Sully Bay is a beach of rocks, pebbles, low-tide mud and a few small patches of sand, backed by a coastal path. Two free parking areas are located at grid ref: ST 152679 (GPS: 51.4037°N, 3.2209°W) and ST 157677 (GPS: 51.4035°N, 3.2166°W). From the first, beach access is down a slipway. The photo opposite shows the view towards Sully Island.

Bendricks Beach

GRID REF **ST 133670**
GPS **51.3949°N, 3.2463°W**
COUNTY **Vale of Glamorgan**
BEACH FACES **South**

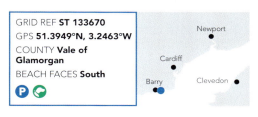

Located between Bendrick Rock and Hayes Point, Bendricks Beach is a small cove of sandstone rocks, some sand and plenty of low-tide mud. Backed by Sully's Atlantic Trading estate, roadside parking can be found here just behind the beach. Access to the shore is a short path across some rough ground and down the remains of a slipway. Look out for the shallow depressions in the bedrock to the west of the slipway, which have been identified as dinosaur footprints.

Jackson's Bay

GRID REF **ST 122665**
GPS **51.3902°N, 3.2620°W**
COUNTY **Vale of Glamorgan**
BEACH FACES **South-east**

Jackson's Bay is a small, sheltered beach to the east of Barry Island's more popular Whitmore Bay. Access is along paths either around Nell's Point from Whitmore Bay or from nearby Redbrink Crescent. The sandy shore is bounded on the eastern side by a stone breakwater and backed by low cliffs of sandstone and mudstone. Barry Island Railway Station is half a mile away and seasonal toilets are located behind the beach. High-tide swimming is generally safe within the bay, but strong offshore currents occur around Nell's Point.

Barry Island (Whitmore Bay)

GRID REF **ST 115663**
GPS **51.3883°N, 3.2720°W**
COUNTY **Vale of Glamorgan**
BEACH FACES **South**

Barry Island's Whitmore Bay is a favourite seaside destination for the population of Cardiff and the Valleys. The sandy beach is backed by a promenade, and can get very crowded. Access is down steps or slipways. Swimming within the bay is generally safe, but there are strong currents just outside. Facilities include toilets, showers, drinking water, cafes, a Tourist Information Centre and a fairground.

A pay & display car park is located just off the A4055. Barry Island Railway Station is a five-minute walk from the beach and has a frequent service to Cardiff. Lifeguards patrol during the summer and a dog ban applies from 1 May to 30 September.

Watch House Bay

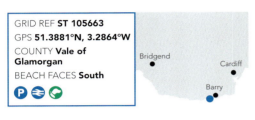

GRID REF **ST 105663**
GPS **51.3881°N, 3.2864°W**
COUNTY **Vale of Glamorgan**
BEACH FACES **South**

Watch House Bay (also known as Watch Tower Bay) is what remains of the channel which once

separated Barry Island from the mainland. This sandy beach has some rock pools to explore and a breakwater on the east side, but the back of the beach has become silted.

Barry Island's main pay & display car park is at the north-east corner, from where a level path of about 360 metres leads to the beach. Parking on the west (Cold Knap Point) side is difficult, but the railway stations of Barry and Barry Island are both within easy walking distance.

Cold Knap

GRID REF **ST 098663**
GPS **51.3880°N, 3.2964°W**
COUNTY **Vale of Glamorgan**
BEACH FACES **South-east**

Cold Knap beach consists of a steep storm bank of pebbles, with some sand at low tide. A car park runs along the back of the beach,

but parking on the pebbles is not allowed. To the west the pebble bank is backed by limestone cliffs, around which gryphaea and ammonite fossils can be found. Heading east, the section of the beach which leads to Cold Knap Point is subject to dog restrictions from 1 May to 30 September. Beach facilities include toilets, a cold water shower and usually a catering van. Barry Railway Station is three quarters of a mile away.

Porthkerry

GRID REF **ST 087665**
GPS **51.3896°N, 3.3123°W**
COUNTY **Vale of Glamorgan**
BEACH FACES **South-east**

Reaching from Bulwarks Iron Age Hill Fort at the west side to Bullnose Cliff at the east, Porthkerry Beach consists of a storm bank of

limestone pebbles with some low-tide sand. Behind the beach is Porthkerry Country Park, set in a valley which the stream of Whitelands Brook meanders along. This is crossed by an impressive thirty-three-metre-high stone railway viaduct. Cold Knap can be easily reached along the shore or via the cliff path.

Access to the shore is a mostly level walk of 250 metres along paths. Facilities include a cafe, toilets, picnic benches, a play area, woodland walks and a pitch & putt golf course.

Rhoose Point

GRID REF **ST 067655**
GPS **51.3803°N, 3.3408°W**
COUNTY **Vale of Glamorgan**
BEACH FACES **South**

At Rhoose Point the limestone cliffs have been breached by quarrying. The former quarries now host a housing estate and a Nature Reserve, the latter giving easy access to the shore through the breach in the cliffs. The beach is rocky with no sand, and swimming is dangerous.

Fontygary Bay

GRID REF **ST 052658**
GPS **51.3828°N, 3.3624°W**
COUNTY **Vale of Glamorgan**
BEACH FACES **South**

Fontygary Bay is a rocky beach with some low-tide sand, backed by unstable cliffs of Blue Lias. Parking is available at Fontygary Bay Holiday Park, and access to the shore is a short walk down some concrete steps.

The nearby village of Rhoose has a pub and a railway station. A public footpath leads directly south to the coastal path, which can be followed in a westerly direction to the beach. The total distance is just under three quarters of a mile.

Leys Beach

GRID REF **ST 037658**
GPS **51.3825°N, 3.3840°W**
COUNTY **Vale of Glamorgan**
BEACH FACES **South**

Leys is one of the best beaches on this section of coast, with some good areas of sand, small dunes, pebbles and groynes. A good place for sunbathing, there's plenty to explore in the derelict lime works, a small pond and the Aberthaw Biodiversity Area behind. The Thaw emerges on to the beach in front of Aberthaw Power Station and Leys Beach is immediately east of this. Still further east is Watch House Beach. The seawater is usually a muddy brown colour, and strong currents render it unsuitable for swimming.

Limpert Bay

GRID REF **ST 019662**
GPS **51.3858°N, 3.4099°W**
COUNTY **Vale of Glamorgan**
BEACH FACES **South**

Lying south-west of Breaksea Point and overlooked by Aberthaw Power Station, Limpert Bay is a beach of rocks and some patches of low-tide sand, backed by a storm bank of pebbles. Access is from the village of Gileston along a narrow lane enticingly signposted 'Beach'. A free car park is situated behind the pebble bank, between the power station and the ruins of a cottage.

Summerhouse Point (Penry Bay)

GRID REF **SS 996663**
GPS **51.3863°N, 3.4430°W**
COUNTY **Vale of Glamorgan**
BEACH FACES **South**

The beach at Summerhouse Point consists almost entirely of rocks, pebbles and wave-cut platforms, with only minuscule amounts of sand showing at low tide. Backed by unstable cliffs of Blue Lias, it looks out across the Bristol Channel

to Minehead (straight across) and Porlock Bay (to the right).

To get there from the village of Llantwit Major, follow Mill Road towards Summerhouse Point, going along a track for the last half a mile. At the far end is a secluded parking area, and from here a footpath continues to the coastal path, passing the overgrown ramparts of Summerhouse Camp, an Iron Age promontory fort. Proceeding eastwards will lead on to the shore at Penry Bay, where the coastal path continues along the back of the beach.

Llantwit Major

GRID REF **SS 955673**
GPS **51.3946°N, 3.5022°W**
COUNTY **Vale of Glamorgan**
BEACH FACES **South**

Situated at the end of the Colhuw valley, Llantwit Major beach has a mix of shingle, rocks and sand. The surrounding cliffs are made up of alternating layers of limestone and shale, and are very unstable. Half a mile to the east is a good place for fossil collecting, gastropods and

gryphaea being common finds.

The main car park overlooks the shore, and further parking is available on grass at peak times. Beach facilities include picnic tables, cycle stands, toilets and a cafe. A dog ban operates from 1 May to 30 September, and RNLI lifeguards patrol from the end of June until early September. This is also a popular spot for windsurfing and surfing – the surf working best at low to mid tide – but due to rocks, rip currents and a hint of localism, it's not ideal for beginners.

Llantwit Major village is just under a mile away and has cafes, pubs, shops, a sports centre and a railway station.

Tresilian Bay

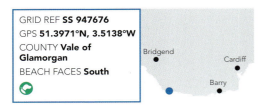

GRID REF **SS 947676**
GPS **51.3971°N, 3.5138°W**
COUNTY **Vale of Glamorgan**
BEACH FACES **South**

Tresilian Bay is a small cove of rocks and some low-tide sand backed by a storm bank of pebbles. Tresilian House sits in the small valley just behind the beach. Although the Blue Lias cliffs to either side of the bay are very unstable, they do have some caves, with Reynard's Cave on the west side the largest.

Access is from the coastal path, which runs along the pebble bank, and parking is either at St Donat's or Llantwit Major.

St Donat's Bay

GRID REF **SS 935677**
GPS **51.3978°N, 3.5311°W**
COUNTY **Vale of Glamorgan**
BEACH FACES **South**

fortified gateway of Atlantic College. The Blue Lias cliffs to either side are very unstable. Lay-by parking for about eight cars can be found east of St Donat's village alongside the wall of the college grounds at grid ref: SS 940682 (GPS: 51.4030°N, 3.5249°W). From here a footpath leads through a narrow kissing gate and past the sports pitches to the coastal path, which can be followed for about 350 metres in a westerly direction to the beach.

St Donat's Bay is a small beach of rocks, pebbles and low-tide sand backed by a sea wall and the

Marcross (Nash Point)

GRID REF **SS 914683**
GPS **51.4028°N, 3.5614°W**
COUNTY **Vale of Glamorgan**
BEACH FACES **South-east**

The beach at Marcross is completely rocky, but better sandy areas can be found (tide permitting) around Nash Point to the west. The attended car park on the clifftop is reached along a private road from Marcross village and beach access from here is down the steep-sided Cwm Marcross valley. Be aware of the surrounding limestone cliffs, which are very unstable, and the sheer drops from the parking area to the shore. Behind the beach a footpath follows the wooded valley to Marcross village, which has a pub.

1 Monknash Beach **2** Monknash Beach, the way on to the beach

Monknash

GRID REF **SS 903700**
GPS **51.4178°N, 3.5778°W**
COUNTY **Vale of Glamorgan**
BEACH FACES **South-east**

Once known as Traeth yr Aes, Monknash is a beach of rocks, wave-cut shore platforms and some low-tide sand, backed by unstable cliffs of Blue Lias.

Just south of Monknash village is the Plough and Harrow pub, from where a lane leads to a car park at grid ref: SS 912700 (GPS: 51.4180°N, 3.5648°W). From the car park, continue along the lane, turning left on to a footpath through the Blaen-Y-Cwm Nature Reserve which then leads on to the beach. Alternatively, roadside parking is possible at the junction with Water Street, from where a good public footpath leads across several stone stiles, closely following Nash Brook to the Nature Reserve and beach.

Wick Beach

GRID REF **SS 896718**
GPS **51.4339°N, 3.5884°W**
COUNTY **Vale of Glamorgan**
BEACH FACES **South-east**

Wick is a remote sandy beach, reached by public footpath from the Monknash Road west of Wick. Some limited space for roadside parking can be found at grid ref: SS 911720 (GPS: 51.4360°N, 3.5669°W), and from here a public footpath leads across three fields to a gully. Final access to the shore is by means of two steel ladders. Despite the sixty-metre unstable cliffs it's worth the effort to get here, as this is one of the largest areas of sand on this part of the coast. However, being rather isolated, it's popular with local naturists.

Temple Bay

GRID REF **SS 889726**
GPS **51.4409°N, 3.5987°W**
COUNTY **Vale of Glamorgan**
BEACH FACES **South-east**

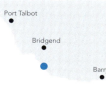

Temple Bay is a secret, sheltered beach of sand, wave-cut platforms and rock pools. The closest parking is at Southerndown Beach. From here, follow the coastal path eastwards past the site of Dunraven Castle (a mansion house demolished in the 1960s) and a walled garden which is open to the public. Further along is a viewpoint of the Heritage Coast towards Nash Point, and Temple Bay is directly below.

To reach the shore, turn right at the viewpoint and left up some steps, after which a steep path descends to the shore. This path can be cut off by the incoming tide. The next closest egress from the shore is at Wick Beach, two thirds of a mile to the east.

Southerndown (Dunraven Bay)

GRID REF **SS 885730**
GPS **51.4445°N, 3.6046°W**
COUNTY **Vale of Glamorgan**
BEACH FACES **South-east**

Once known as Seamouth, Southerndown Beach is one of the better beaches on the Glamorgan Coast and is part of the Southerndown Coast SSSI. Bounded on the eastern side by the headland of Witches Point, this sandy beach is full of small streams and rock pools, and is backed by a pebble bank and unstable limestone cliffs.

An attended car park overlooks the bay, and further parking on grass is available at peak times. A dog ban operates from May to September inclusive, and beach facilities include toilets, a picnic area, a Heritage Coast Visitor Centre and a beach shop. Swimming is generally safe inshore, but there are strong currents near Witches Point and RNLI lifeguards patrol during the school summer holidays.

A reef to the right means this is a popular surf beach, with the best conditions between low and mid tide. However, be wary of submerged rocks, which become a problem as the tide nears the shingle.

Ogmore-by-Sea

GRID REF **SS 860752**
GPS **51.4637°N, 3.6413°W**
COUNTY **Vale of Glamorgan**
BEACH FACES **South-east**

Ogmore-by-Sea lies east of the Ogmore river at the western end of the Glamorgan Heritage Coast. The beach is sandy at low tide, with some pebbles and backed by low cliffs of carboniferous limestone. A pay & display car park with toilets is located just above the beach, where the parking is mainly on grass, and access to the shore is down a new concrete slipway.

Lifeguards patrol from late June until early September.

At low tide the river can be crossed to reach the beach and the sand dunes of Merthyr Mawr, but bathing in the river is prohibited due to currents.

East of Ogmore Beach is an area of wave-cut platforms indented with small coves. The first and largest of these is Bwlch Gwyn, a steeply sloping beach of shingle, streams and rock pools, to which access is down a worse-for-wear slipway. Further east are Bwlch Kate Antony and Bwlch y Gro. Once a hazard to shipping but now a popular diving location, the tidal reef of Tusker Rock lies just over a mile offshore.

Merthyr Mawr Beach

GRID REF **SS 856764**
GPS **51.4744°N, 3.6474°W**
COUNTY **Bridgend**
BEACH FACES **South-west**

Merthyr Mawr is a wide, sandy beach. Ogmore Castle is just a short walk along a public footpath from the idyllic village of Merthyr Mawr, the public footpath crossing the Ogmore and Ewenny rivers by means of a small suspension footbridge and stepping stones respectively.

A pay & display car park is pleasantly situated next to the ruins of Candleston Castle at grid ref: SS 871772 (GPS: 51.4828°N, 3.6267°W), and can be reached by following a lane through Merthyr Mawr village. A small wooden hut houses male and female toilets. One of the largest sand dunes in Europe – known locally as the Big Dipper – is just south of the car park. Candleston Castle was a fourteenth-century fortified manor house, reputedly haunted, and was allegedly once part of a lost village called Treganlaw, now believed to be buried under the shifting sands.

Access to the beach is a walk of three quarters of a mile across the dunes of Merthyr Mawr warren. The dune system is a maze of paths with numerous ways to the shore, but the main route is waymarked. It's thirsty work on a hot day, so bring plenty of drinks. Alternative access to the beach is by wading across the river at low to mid tide from the car parks at Ogmore. Swimming is generally safe away from the river.

Newton Bay

GRID REF **SS 838767**
GPS **51.4768°N, 3.6734°W**
COUNTY **Bridgend**
BEACH FACES **South-east**

Newton Bay (also known as Black Rock Beach) is the most easterly of Porthcawl's beaches. The shore is sand backed by some shingle and low dunes, becoming rocky towards Newton Point. The extensive Trecco Bay Holiday Park is on the west side, and to the east the dunes and sandy shore continue to Merthyr Mawr Beach.

A pay & display car park overlooks the shore, and roadside parking can be found nearby. Access is then down a slipway.

Trecco Bay

GRID REF **SS 832764**
GPS **51.4740°N, 3.6819°W**
COUNTY **Bridgend**
BEACH FACES **South**

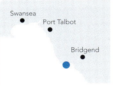

The sandy beach of Trecco Bay is backed by a sea wall and dunes, behind which is Trecco Bay's extensive caravan park. Access is down ramps or steps. Parking is available at Newton Point, but reaching the car park involves driving through the holiday park. Some roadside parking can be found on Rhych Avenue, at grid ref: SS 829768 (GPS: 51.4783°N, 3.6876°W).

A dog ban operates from May to September inclusive and lifeguards patrol during summer. As rip currents often occur near Newton Point, bathing is prohibited in this area.

Sandy Bay (Coney Beach)

GRID REF **SS 825765**
GPS **51.4747°N, 3.6921°W**
COUNTY **Bridgend**
BEACH FACES **South**

Swansea
Port Talbot
Bridgend

Sandy Bay lies between Porthcawl harbour and Rhych Point. At the town end it's backed by a sea wall, a fairground and numerous fast food outlets. A large pay & display car park can be found on this side, in addition to plenty of roadside parking. Low dunes back the east side of the bay, and from May to September lifeguards patrol and a dog ban operates. Surfing is best at mid to high tide on the eastern side of the beach. The harbour wall provides some shelter, making it a good choice when beaches further west are too rough. Rip currents can occur at either end in surf conditions.

Porthcawl Town Beach & Hutchwns Beach

Porthcawl Town Beach

GRID REF **SS 814764**
GPS **51.4736°N, 3.7079°W**
COUNTY **Bridgend**
BEACH FACES **South**

Hutchwns Beach

GRID REF **SS 810767**
GPS **51.4762°N, 3.7137°W**
COUNTY **Bridgend**
BEACH FACES **South**

Porthcawl Town Beach (also known as Seafront Beach) lies west of Porthcawl harbour. Backed by a promenade, it's a beach of limestone rocks and some small areas of sand, but part of the upper shore has been tarmacked to prevent erosion. Access is down steps or a slipway, and swimming is prohibited due to dangerous currents. There are plenty of facilities nearby and in the town centre, including toilets, cafes and takeaways, and there are dog restrictions from May to September inclusive.

Also known as the Pipe Beach, Hutchwns Beach is further west, just before Hutchwns Point. Backed by a sea wall, it's a similar beach of limestone rocks, small sandy areas and some low-tide sand. Access involves walking over rocks from either end.

Rest Bay & Pink Bay

Rest Bay

GRID REF **SS 803780**
GPS **51.4877°N, 3.7242°W**
COUNTY **Bridgend**
BEACH FACES **South-west**

Pink Bay

GRID REF **SS 795792**
GPS **51.4983°N, 3.7362°W**
COUNTY **Bridgend**
BEACH FACES **South-west**

Swansea
Port Talbot
Bridgend

On the western side of Porthcawl, Rest Bay is a sandy beach with some pebbles, backed by limestone rocks. Lifeguards patrol from late May until early September, and a dog ban operates from 1 May to 30 September. Beach facilities include toilets, a cafe, showers and drinking water. Access is down a slipway from a pay & display car park.

This is a popular beach for surfing and windsurfing, and is generally suitable for beginners. Watch out for a strong rip in the direction of the town which occurs near the point of the beach after mid tide on a rising tide. Surfers are advised to keep to the north-west side of the lifeguard station until the tide is clear of the point.

Pink Bay is at the north-western end of Rest Bay, and is a similar sandy beach backed by a bank of pebbles and the Wales Coastal Path. It gets its name from the pink marbling effect of the pebbles. This is also a good surfing beach, at its best towards the high tide.

24

4 Kenfig Sands, from the northern end   **5** Kenfig Sands

Kenfig Sands (Sker Beach)

GRID REF **SS 783810**
GPS **51.5143°N, 3.7541°W**
COUNTY **Bridgend**
BEACH FACES **South-west**

Kenfig Sands, or Sker Beach, is a two-mile stretch of sand reaching from Sker Point at the southern end to the Kenfig river. Beyond the river, the sandy shore continues northwards as Margam Sands. For most of its length, it's backed by a shingle bank and the dunes of Kenfig National Nature Reserve.

At Kenfig village, a visitor centre for the reserve has plenty of free parking, cycle stands and some picnic tables. The beach is approximately a mile away and there are many paths and possible routes, some of which become impassable or boggy, so it's best to follow the marked rights of way. Alternative access is along the coastal path from Rest Bay.

A lifeguard station is manned by volunteers during weekends and summer bank holidays. Surf conditions are best on a rising (but not high) tide, with fairly consistent surf. However, there can be strong rips and it's not one for the inexperienced.

Margam Sands (Morfa Beach)

GRID REF **SS 773845**
GPS **51.5455°N, 3.7697°W**
COUNTY **Neath Port Talbot**
BEACH FACES **West**

Margam Sands, or Morfa Beach, is a two-and-a-half-mile beach stretching from the Kenfig river to Port Talbot harbour. The shore is fine sand backed by dunes. Part of the beach is privately owned by the steel works which backs on to its north-western end. Despite this it is a good beach for fishing, surfing and windsurfing, with surf conditions best towards the high tide. About 230 metres from Port Talbot harbour are the remains of the *SS Amazon*, wrecked in 1908.

To get there, take the road heading west from Junction 38 of the M4 (Heolcae'r Bont) and follow it to Margam Moors level crossing, where there is some space for parking. It's advisable not to leave valuables in your car here. Access to the shore is by crossing the railway and following a narrow lane for about a mile.

Aberavon Sands & Baglan Beach

Aberavon Sands

GRID REF **SS 745894**

GPS **51.5889°N, 3.8118°W**

COUNTY **Neath Port Talbot**

BEACH FACES **South-east**

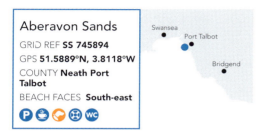

Aberavon Sands is a long beach of sand and a few patches of low-tide mud, stretching two and a half miles from Witford Point to Port Talbot docks. The southern end is known as Aberavon Beach and is backed by a sea wall and promenade. Dog restrictions apply from 1 May to 30 September. To the north-west, the sea wall gives way to sand dunes – this end is known as Baglan Beach and dogs are allowed here. Access to Aberavon Beach is down steps or a slipway, and lifeguards patrol from the end of May until early September.

Facilities include toilets, a cafe, a children's paddling pool and play area. Roadside parking is available, in addition to pay & display car parks. Surf conditions are best between mid and high tide, with the far southern end near the harbour being the favoured zone, but a rip current often occurs here.

The Gower Peninsula lies west of Swansea, and is an Area of Outstanding Natural Beauty. The landscape is dotted with castles and other ancient monuments. Its geology is predominantly Carboniferous Limestone, with Millstone Grit at Oxwich and Old Red Sandstone at Rhossili Down, the Gower Peninsula's highest point.

Along the southern shore are the popular sandy beaches of Langland, Caswell, Three Cliffs, Oxwich and Port Eynon. West of Port Eynon the coast becomes rocky with spectacular limestone cliffs. At the south-west corner of Gower, the Worm's Head Peninsula can be reached by a low-tide causeway. The northern coast has no beaches to speak of.

Gower roads tend to be narrow and winding, and slow journeys can be expected at peak times. However, it's worth exploring the area on foot on the well-maintained public footpaths. Lifeguards patrol the main beaches in summer.

SWANSEA & GOWER

Opposite Fall Bay

Jersey Marine Beach

GRID REF **SS 703925**
GPS **51.6158°N, 3.8735°W**
COUNTY **Swansea**
BEACH FACES **South**

Also known as Crymlyn Beach, Jersey Marine is a two-mile, little-visited beach between Swansea docks and the River Neath. The sandy shore is backed by dunes and the Crymlyn Bog Nature Reserve. The tide can go out over a mile and hazards of the beach include mud, strong currents near the river estuary and extensive sandbanks on a low tide. It's a good choice for shell collecting – likely finds include razor shells, carpet shells, trough shells, slipper limpets, whelks, oysters, cockles, scallops and mussels. Dogs are allowed at all times, and the beach is popular with local dog walkers.

Roadside parking is available on Elba Crescent, just off the A483 (Fabian Way) at the Swansea Gate Business Park junction, north side at grid ref: SS 704930 (GPS: 51.6221°N, 3.8738°W). Beach access is then a walk of 650 metres along a sandy path from the junction.

2 Swansea Bay, at Sketty **3** Swansea Bay **4** Black Pill, towards Mumbles

Swansea Bay

GRID REF **SS 621907**
GPS **51.5977°N, 3.9912°W**
COUNTY **Swansea**
BEACH FACES **South-east**

Swansea Bay extends four miles from the River Tawe to Mumbles Point. The upper shore is mostly sandy as far as Oystermouth, beyond which it becomes stony. The lower shore has patches of mud, and at low tide you're unlikely to reach the sea without sinking at least to your ankles. The beach can be enjoyed by bike as well, as a promenade/cyclepath runs behind its length. Mumbles Point and Mumbles Pier are at the far western end of the bay.

Dog restrictions apply on two sections of the beach from 1 May to 30 September: from the River Tawe to the slip opposite Victoria Park and from the access point at Sketty Lane to the slip opposite the West Cross Inn. Facilities along the bay include:

» **St Helen's** – pay & display car park, toilets, and lifeguards during the school summer holidays.
» **Sketty Lane** – pay & display car park, Singleton Park (boating lake and pub), the fifty-metre Wales National Pool, and level access to the beach.
» **Black Pill** – pay & display car park (on the north side of road), a restaurant, toilets, children's paddling pool and play area.
» **Oystermouth** – pay & display car park, a shopping street, toilets and Oystermouth Castle.

Mumbles Beach

GRID REF **SS 621907**
GPS **51.5977°N, 3.9912°W**
COUNTY **Swansea**
BEACH FACES **South-east**

Between Mumbles Point and the pier is a small sandy beach backed by a concrete sea wall. Access is down a flight of concrete steps from the pier, or alternatively by walking around the point from Bracelet Bay at low tide.

Bracelet Bay

GRID REF **SS 631873**
GPS **51.5674°N, 3.9755°W**
COUNTY **Swansea**
BEACH FACES **South**

Bracelet Bay is the first beach west of Mumbles Point, and has a shore of limestone rocks, pebbles and some sand. Swimming is inadvisable due to strong currents just offshore. The beach is served by a frequent bus service from Swansea, and access is down a steep path. Facilities include a large pay & display car park overlooking the beach, a bar/restaurant and toilets. A dog ban operates from May to September inclusive and lifeguards patrol during the summer school holidays.

Limeslade Bay

GRID REF **SS 625870**
GPS **51.5646°N, 3.9840°W**
COUNTY **Swansea**
BEACH FACES **South**

Limeslade is a small bay of rocks, pebbles and some low-tide sand to the west of Mumbles Point. A pay & display car park overlooks the beach and a frequent bus service operates from Swansea. Facilities include toilets, a bar/restaurant and an ice cream parlour. Access is down a flight of steps, and a dog ban applies from May to September inclusive.

Rotherslade & Langland Bay

GRID REF **SS 607872**
GPS **51.5659°N, 4.0100°W**
COUNTY **Swansea**
BEACH FACES **South**

Llanelli

Swansea

The sandy bay of Langland regularly attains the Blue Flag Award, and is one of the busiest beaches on Gower due to its proximity to Swansea. About a quarter of a mile wide, it lies east of Snaple Point and is backed by some shingle, a sea wall and a promenade. Facilities include cafes, beach shops, tennis courts and toilets. Parking is at a pay & display car park and access to the shore is down steps or a slipway.

From May until early September, lifeguards patrol the beach and a complete dog ban is in place. A popular surf beach, it's good at most stages of the tide and generally suitable for beginners. However, it can get very crowded and there are a few rocks to watch for. Localism can also be a problem. The eastern end of the beach is known as Rotherslade, which has additional toilets. This becomes a small cove at high tide, and another smaller cove can be found further to the east.

3 Caswell Bay

Caswell Bay

GRID REF **SS 593875**
GPS **51.5683°N, 4.0303°W**
COUNTY **Swansea**
BEACH FACES **South**

Caswell, on the south-east side of the Gower Peninsula, is a very popular bay due to its proximity to Swansea. The sandy beach is flanked by limestone cliffs and regularly attains the Blue Flag Award. At low tide it's about 650 metres wide, but around high tide beach space is very limited. Be sure to check the tide times before visiting, especially during hot weather.

A pay & display car park is located in the valley behind the beach, behind which is the Bishop's Wood Nature Reserve. Access to the shore is down steps or a slipway. Beach facilities include toilets, a cafe, beach shops and cold water showers. Lifeguards patrol from May until early September, and a dog ban applies from May to September inclusive.

This is a very popular surfing beach, surfable at most stages of the tide, but mid to high tide is best. Usually suitable for beginners, it can get crowded, and a rip current can occur on the west side in surf conditions.

Brandy Cove

GRID REF **SS 585874**
GPS **51.5672°N, 4.0418°W**
COUNTY **Swansea**
BEACH FACES **South**

Lying just west of Caswell Bay, Brandy Cove is a small beach of sand and rock pools, backed by pebbles and flanked by low limestone cliffs and caves. Galena (lead ore) was once mined here, and the gated entrance to the All Slade mine can be seen at the back of the beach. Parking is either at Caswell Bay or at Pyle Corner, Bishopston. The coastal path is about half a mile from the latter and is reached along the appropriately named Brandy Cove Road, which leads to a wide footpath. Final beach access is a short, steep path with steps.

Many legends are associated with this beach. As its name suggests, it was, together with neighbouring Pwlldu Bay, a haven for smugglers in the eighteenth century who landed cargoes of tobacco and alcohol. Another tale is that of a haggard woman known as Old Moll who lived in the caves. Supposedly a witch, she was thought to bring disease and misfortune wherever she went. The beach was also the scene of a murder in 1919 – the victim's remains being hidden behind boulders in the mine where they remained undiscovered until 1961.

Pwlldu Bay

GRID REF **SS 576870**
GPS **51.5634°N, 4.0546°W**
COUNTY **Swansea**
BEACH FACES **South**

Once a haven for smugglers and later a centre for limestone quarrying, Pwlldu is now a secluded National Trust bay south of Bishopston. The sandy beach is backed by a storm bank of pebbles and flanked by limestone cliffs.

At high tide it's approximately 275 metres wide, extending to the east and becoming half a mile wide on the low tide. This part of the beach is known as Seven Slades.

Swimming within the bay is generally safe, and a pebble bank has partially blocked a stream, forming a pool behind the beach ('Pwlldu' translates as 'black pool'). The closest parking is at Pyle Corner, Bishopston at grid ref: SS 580882 (GPS: 51.5740°N, 4.0490°W), from where Pwlldu Lane leads to the clifftop, thence becoming a track down the eastern side – a total distance of about a mile.

Bantam Bay

GRID REF **SS 574866**
GPS **51.5597°N, 4.0574°W**
COUNTY **Swansea**
BEACH FACES **South**

Bantam Bay is a small, little-known bay of rocks and low-tide sand, backed by limestone cliffs. Located just around the western point from Pwlldu Bay, it can be reached by walking along Pwlldu's rocky western shore. Some scrambling is required to get past the point. A little further west in a gully is a lugubrious circle of stones known as Grave's End, where around sixty-five press-ganged sailors from the *Caesar*, wrecked in November 1760, were buried.

Hunts Bay

GRID REF **SS 563868**
GPS **51.5612°N, 4.0733°W**
COUNTY **Swansea**
BEACH FACES **South**

Hunts Bay, also known as Deep Slade, lies between the headlands of High Tor and Pwlldu Head. Once a sandy beach, it's now a bay of limestone rocks, shingle and small patches of gravelly sand, backed by low boulder clay cliffs. Parking is half a mile to the west in the village of Southgate at grid ref: SS 553874 (GPS: 51.5668°N, 4.0881°W). Around the point to the west is Bacon Hole, one of the Gower's largest caves. It can be found by walking around the point at low tide, and up the steeply sloping rocks towards an overhang, which is the cave's entrance.

Foxhole

GRID REF **SS 553870**
GPS **51.5628°N, 4.0878°W**
COUNTY **Swansea**
BEACH FACES **South**

Lying below the village of Southgate, Foxhole is a small, sandy beach backed by rocks and high limestone cliffs which divides into two smaller coves around mid tide. Access from Southgate is down steep paths. Facilities at the village include a National Trust pay & display car park and a coffee shop with toilets.

To the east of Foxhole is the headland of High Tor, beneath which lies Minchin Hole. Forty-five metres long and above the high water mark, it can be reached at most stages of the tide. To find it take the steep path descending the west side of the tor, then skirting around to the east. A deep zawn leads to its entrance.

Pobbles Bay & Three Cliffs Bay

Pobbles Bay

GRID REF **SS 540877**
GPS **51.5687°N, 4.1068°W**
COUNTY **Swansea**
BEACH FACES **South**

To the east of the distinctive headland of Three Cliffs Bay lies Pobbles Bay, a beach of sand backed by high limestone cliffs, which provide good shelter for sunbathing. Access is via the coastal path from Southgate (about three quarters of a mile away) – a mostly level walk followed by a steep sandy descent. Alternatively, a public footpath beginning at Pennard Golf Club leads directly to Pobbles Bay. There are no facilities at the beach, but Southgate has a National Trust pay & display car park on the clifftop, a coffee shop and toilets.

Three Cliffs Bay is west of the headland and one of Gower's most picturesque beaches. The shore is mostly sand, with dunes, high limestone cliffs and a pebble bank. The Pennard Pill snakes its way across the bay and can cause rip currents on an ebbing tide. Dangerous rips also occur in surf conditions, but otherwise swimming is generally safe. Just inland on the eastern side are the ruins of Pennard Castle.

The closest parking is at Penmaen, either in a busy lay-by on the south side of the road, or on the north side just across the cattle grid on Cefn Bryn common at grid ref: SS 526885 (GPS: 51.5761°N, 4.1274°W). Public footpaths then lead to Three Cliffs and also to Tor Bay. Lifeguards patrol in summer during weekends and school holidays.

Tor Bay

GRID REF **SS 528877**
GPS **51.5684°N, 4.1241°W**
COUNTY **Swansea**
BEACH FACES **South**

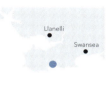

Tor Bay is a sheltered sandy beach at the eastern end of Oxwich Bay (overleaf), lying between the limestone headlands of Great Tor and Little Tor. The nearest parking is at Penmaen, at grid ref: SS 526885 (GPS: 51.5758°N, 4.1284°W), either at a lay-by on the south side of the road, or on Cefn Bryn Common just across the cattle grid on the north side. A public footpath then leads to the coastal path on the clifftop, from where access to the shore is down a steep, sandy path. The beach is at its best between high and mid tide.

Crawley Beach

GRID REF **SS 525877**
GPS **51.5683°N, 4.1285°W**
COUNTY **Swansea**
BEACH FACES **South**

Also known as Nicholaston Beach, Crawley Beach is a wide, sandy beach situated at the eastern end of Oxwich Bay, and is backed by the dunes of Nicholaston Burrows. The closest parking is at Penmaen (as for Three Cliffs Bay), from where good footpaths lead to Tor Bay, Crawley and Three Cliffs. Alternative parking for about six cars can be found on the north side of the road about a mile further on, just before St Nicholas Church. From here, a public footpath leads to Nicholaston Woods, descending to the dunes of Nicholaston Burrows.

Oxwich Bay

GRID REF **SS 505866**
GPS **51.5579°N, 4.1568°W**
COUNTY **Swansea**
BEACH FACES **South-east**

At Oxwich, Gower's limestone cliffs give way to softer Millstone Grit. The resulting erosion from the sea has formed Oxwich Bay, a two-mile long sandy beach backed by the Oxwich Burrows Nature Reserve. An attended car park overlooks the western end of the beach, and facilities include a slipway, toilets, drinking water and a cafe.

Oxwich Point shelters the bay from westerly winds, and it's generally suitable for swimming, paddleboarding and kayaking. Surf conditions can be good in winter when other beaches blow out, the best time being an hour or two before the high tide.

Slade Sands

GRID REF **SS 487854**
GPS **51.5467°N, 4.1823°W**
COUNTY **Swansea**
BEACH FACES **South**

Slade Sands is a quiet sandy beach about three quarters of a mile east of Port Eynon. The shore is of sand, rocks and rock pools, backed by very low cliffs and fields. Access is via the coastal path from Horton or along the shore at low tide. Alternative access is by footpath from the nearby village of Slade, but parking here is difficult.

Horton & Port Eynon

Port Eynon
GRID REF **SS 469851**
GPS **51.5435°N, 4.2081°W**
COUNTY **Swansea**
BEACH FACES **South-east**

The sandy bay of Port Eynon is backed mostly by dunes. The shore in front of the village is known as Port Eynon, and the eastern end as Horton. East of Horton the shore becomes rocky, with plenty of rock pools. It's generally safe for swimming, and lifeguards patrol from late May until early September. Both Port Eynon and Horton have pay & display car parks and toilets, and Port Eynon has a pub, a surf shop, a campsite and a slipway. Dog restrictions apply from the steps to the beach at Port Eynon to the eastern edge of the access at Horton from May to September.

On the west side of Port Eynon Bay are the remains of the Salt House, where salt was extracted from seawater. Further west is Salt House Mere, a 200-metre-wide secluded cove of sand and rocks. The shore beyond Salt House Mere is completely rocky.

Overton Mere

GRID REF **SS 464848**
GPS **51.5406°N, 4.2152°W**
COUNTY **Swansea**
BEACH FACES **South**

Lying to the west of Port Eynon Point, Overton Mere is a wide bay of limestone rocks, rock pools, shingle and a few tiny patches of sand. A path skirts the back of the beach, providing relatively easy access to the shore. Various bits of nautical wreckage are scattered amongst the rocks, most of it from the tug boat *Wittezee*, wrecked here on 12 November 1940.

On the eastern side of the bay and about 200 metres west of the point is Culver Hole, a narrow cave sealed off by a twenty-metre wall. This was used as a dovecote and probably also as a smugglers' hideout. Access to the interior is usually possible by crawling under the bottom of the wall, depending on the level of the shingle, or by climbing up to the first opening. Inside some perilous steps set into the wall give access to the higher openings.

On the western side of the bay is a local surf spot known as Sumpter's Reef. As with most reefs along this part of the coast, it works best below mid tide. When it does work it can get busy and rocks are a hazard – definitely not for beginners.

Common Cliff

GRID REF **SS 445853**
GPS **51.5446°N, 4.2428°W**
COUNTY **Swansea**
BEACH FACES **South**

The shore at Common Cliff consists of limestone wave-cut platforms, some shingle and tiny patches of sand. Immediately behind the beach is the Long Hole Cliff Nature Reserve, named after Long Hole Cave which can be found at grid ref: SS 451851

(GPS: 51.5431°N, 4.2347°W). The Wales Coast Path runs a few hundred metres inland and is relatively level, but walkers who follow this route are missing some spectacular scenery. A more interesting path descends Blackhole Gut just to the west and skirts the beaches at the base of the cliffs.

The photo shows the coastline looking towards Worm's Head in the distance. A local surf spot known as Pete's Reef can be seen towards the top, but due to sharp rocks it's not suitable for beginners.

Foxhole Slade

GRID REF **SS 437858**
GPS **51.5489°N, 4.2545°W**
COUNTY **Swansea**
BEACH FACES **South**

Foxhole Slade is a small, rocky cove on the south-western tip of the Gower. There are three caves here: Paviland West Cave, Paviland Cave and Paviland Sea Cave, all approximately twenty to thirty metres long. A low tide is needed to visit them, and a low spring tide is preferable.

A narrow, steep-sided inlet runs into the valley behind, and Paviland Sea Cave is on the west side of this. The more famous Paviland Cave is higher up the rocks on the west side and can only be reached when the tide is low enough to cross the beach. Further west is Paviland West Cave. Prehistoric remains have been found at Paviland Cave, including a Stone Age skeleton dubbed 'the Red Lady of Paviland' which was later established to be that of a young man.

The nearest parking is on Pilton Green Common at grid ref: SS 446871 (GPS: 51.5608°N, 4.2421°W), from where a footpath leads across fields to the coastal path. A steep-sided valley then descends to Foxhole Slade.

Knave Bay

GRID REF **SS 433862**
GPS **51.5524°N, 4.2605°W**
COUNTY **Swansea**
BEACH FACES **South**

On the eastern side of The Knave promontory is a bay of jagged limestone rocks. There is hardly any sand, but it's a popular surf spot because of its reef break, which works best around low tide with a small swell. Access involves a steep descent down one of two gullies from the coastal path.

Also of interest here are two caves: Ogof Wyntog and Ogof Ffynnon Wyntog. The latter usually begins with a sump, but this can dry out in summer leading to a cave over a quarter of a mile long, but not suitable for amateur exploration. Just a few metres seaward, Ogof Wyntog is approximately a hundred metres long and has two entrances. The upper entrance is small, and some crawling is necessary to get through, but after a few metres it opens out into a larger chamber. Another short crawl leads to a further chamber with two passages, one of which descends steeply to the larger of the two sea caves beneath. Access or egress via this cave is possible for about two hours either side of low tide.

A short distance up the cliffs to the east is a rock arch with views out to sea.

Parking is available on Pilton Green Common at grid ref: SS 446871 (GPS: 51.5608°N, 4.2421°W), and a footpath leads across fields to the coastal path. The path ahead leads to Foxhole Slade; The Knave and its beach are 550 metres to the west.

PAVILAND
CAVE

PAVILAND
SEA CAVE

1

2

3

4

THE KNAVE

OGOF WYNTOG ›

5

Ramsgrove

GRID REF **SS 428864**	
GPS **51.5540°N, 4.2677°W**	
COUNTY **Swansea**	
BEACH FACES **South**	

Located at the south-western end of the Gower Peninsula, Ramsgrove is a small cove of limestone pebbles, low-tide sand and rock pools.

Access from the coastal path is along a steep-sided limestone valley. Not listed in most Gower guides, it's usually very quiet.

Parking is available on Pilton Green common at grid ref: SS 446871 (GPS: 51.5608°N, 4.2421°W), from where a footpath leads across several fields to the coastal path. Ramsgrove is to the west, the total distance being about one and three quarter miles.

Butterslade

GRID REF **SS 422868**	
GPS **51.5575°N, 4.2766°W**	
COUNTY **Swansea**	
BEACH FACES **South**	

Butterslade lies to the east of Thurba Head and is a mostly rocky beach with deep rock pools, caves and some small patches of low-tide sand. There are no paths down to the shore, and reaching it involves negotiating the rocks at the back of the beach. Butterslade Cave is on the far west side of the bay and is about thirty metres long. Another cave known as Red Chamber is just east of the beach. This cave is about forty metres long and leads to an adit of a further twenty metres.

Mewslade & Fall Bay

Mewslade
GRID REF **SS 420871**
GPS **51.5601°N, 4.2796°W**
CCUNTY **Swansea**
BEACH FACES **South**

Llanelli

Swansea

Backed by high limestone cliffs, these sandy beaches lie south of Rhossili at the far south-western tip of the Gower Peninsula. On a low tide it's possible to walk along the shore between them, but high tide will cover most of the sand. They're popular beaches for sun-bathing, swimming and surfing – surf conditions being best around low to mid tide with a good swell. Rips and rocks can be a hazard, and they're not suitable for beginners.

The nearest parking is an attended car park at Rhossili, where facilities include toilets, cafes and a surf shop. From the village, public footpaths lead south-east towards the coastal path. Further paths then descend the steep-sided valleys to the bays. Final access to Mewslade is a short walk over rocks, and for Fall Bay (see page 29) it's a short, steep rocky path. Note that adders are quite common on this part of the Gower Peninsula.

Rhossili

GRID REF **SS 413890**
GPS **51.5770°N, 4.2905°W**
COUNTY **Swansea**
BEACH FACES **West**

Rhossili Bay is a three-and-a-half-mile beach at the far western end of the Gower Peninsula, the southern half of which is known as Rhossili, and the northern half as Llangennith. The shore is fine golden sand and some shingle, backed by a grass bank. At the southern end, the promontory of Worm's Head is accessible by a causeway for about two and a half hours either side of low tide. Behind the beach, Rhossili Down is the highest point on Gower at 193 metres, and is a superb place to watch the sun setting over Carmarthen Bay.

Parking is at an attended car park in Rhossili village, from where access to the beach is down a long concrete path with steps. Several wrecks can be seen at low tide, including the barque *Vennerne* (wrecked in 1894) and the much-photographed *Helvetia* (wrecked in 1887). Facilities include toilets, a cafe, a visitor centre and shop, a surf shop and a pub.

2 Llangennith   3 Llangennith, looking north towards Burry Holms

Llangennith

GRID REF **SS 410910**
GPS **51.5949°N, 4.2958°W**
COUNTY **Swansea**
BEACH FACES **West**

Llanelli

Swansea

The northern half of Rhossili Bay is known as Llangennith, and has a shore of fine golden sand backed by dunes. Picking up the Atlantic swells, it's the most consistent surf beach on Gower, good at most stages of the tide and usually suitable for beginners.

The remains of a wooden paddle steamer, the *City of Bristol*, is visible on low tides and can be a hazard to surfers. It ran aground during a storm on 17 November 1840 and its location is approximately opposite the emergence of the stream known as Diles Lake. At the northern end of Llangennith Beach, the tidal islet of Burry Holms is accessible for about two hours either side of low tide. A small sandy cove lies just beyond it.

Parking is available at Hillend campsite at Llangennith, from where beach access is a 200-metre boardwalk across the dunes. Facilities include toilets, an ice cream shop and a coffee shop.

Blue Pool Bay

GRID REF **SS 408931**
GPS **51.6137°N, 4.2996°W**
COUNTY **Swansea**
BEACH FACES **North-west**

Llanelli

Swansea

Blue Pool Bay, also known as Blue Pool Corner, is a secluded bay on the western shore of the Gower Peninsula. At its southern end is the Three Chimneys rock arch where gold doubloons from an eighteenth-century shipwreck have been found, but the beach's main attraction is a large, natural rock pool deep enough to jump into from the rocks above.

The nearest car park is at Broughton at grid ref: SS 416925 (GPS: 51.6096°N, 4.2897°W), reached by taking Burrows Lane at the mini roundabout in Llangennith. It's usually free but a fee may be charged at peak times. The path to Blue Pool is signposted, and final access to the shore involves negotiating a steep path and rocks at the beach's northern end. Although dogs are allowed you may have to assist them down this steep path. It's best to visit within an hour or two of low tide, otherwise the sand will be completely covered. As with neighbouring Broughton Bay, there are strong offshore currents, meaning swimming can be dangerous.

3 Broughton Bay, from the south   **4** Broughton Bay, cove at the south end

Broughton Bay

GRID REF **SS 417935**
GPS **51.6175°N, 4.2868°W**
COUNTY **Swansea**
BEACH FACES **North-west**

Llanelli

Swansea

Located at the far western end of the Gower Peninsula, Broughton Bay (pronounced 'Bruffton') is a beach of clean, fine sand backed by dunes, with caravan parks at both ends.

To the north is Whiteford Sands, which can be reached along the shore at most stages of the tide. A car park is located at Broughton Burrows at grid ref: SS 416925 (GPS: 51.6096°N, 4.2897°W), reached by taking the Broughton exit at the mini roundabout in Llangennith village. Footpaths to Broughton Bay, Blue Pool Corner and Rhossili Bay are well signposted. Surf conditions are best from mid to high tide, especially when Llangennith gets too big, but there can be strong currents and it's not a beach for beginners.

Whiteford Sands

GRID REF **SS 435947**
GPS **51.6288°N, 4.2614°W**
COUNTY **Swansea**
BEACH FACES **North-west**

Situated at the north-western tip of the Gower Peninsula, Whiteford Sands (pronounced 'Whitford') is a two-mile sandy beach backed by dunes and the Nature Reserve of Whiteford Burrows. Just offshore is the Loughor estuary and swimming can be dangerous due to currents, but it's a good choice for sunbathing, escaping the crowds and exploring. Once part of a firing range, signs warn against touching suspicious objects.

Whiteford's cast iron lighthouse stands on a spit at the north end of the beach, and can be reached at low tide. At most stages of the tide

it's possible to walk south along the shore to neighbouring Broughton Bay.

The nearest parking is at Llanmadoc; take the right fork at the church towards Cwm Ivy, and the car park is a few metres down on the right. From here it's a good three-quarters-of-a-mile walk to the beach. Alternatively, park in Llanmadoc village and follow the public footpath marked 'Whiteford Burrows', which leads to the rear of the dunes at the approximate centre point of the beach.

There have been many wrecks along this beach, and following a severe storm in January 1868 the beach was strewn with bodies from wrecked ships. Not surprisingly there are several reports of hauntings, one being the thunder of horses' hooves commencing in the direction of Broughton Bay and ending suddenly at Whiteford.

Llanrhidian Sands

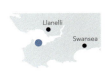

GRID REF **SS 472948**
GPS **51.6307°N, 4.2080°W**
COUNTY **Swansea**
BEACH FACES **North**

Llanrhidian Sands is a large, windswept and mostly featureless expanse of sand on the northern coast of the Gower Peninsula. The shore consists of wet sand and millions of cockle shells (the light area in the photo), backed by salt marsh. The area was once part of a firing range, and a derelict observation

post still stands on the beach. Signs warn not to touch any items of military debris.

From the coastal path below Weobley Castle (pronounced 'Web-lee'), a stone track leads for one and a third miles across Llanrhidian Marsh to the shore. This track is not a right of way, so please don't use without permission. At high tide most of the sand is covered, and spring tides will also cover the salt marsh. It would be wise to check the tide times before visiting, and not to stray too far out on an incoming tide.

Carmarthenshire has a relatively short coastline, but its section of the Wales Coastal Path is sixty-eight miles long, having to make extensive inland detours around the Towy and Taf estuaries. With a length of about seven and a half miles, Pembrey is easily its best beach and is backed by Pembrey Country Park. Inland, Carmarthenshire has some impressive scenery with rolling hills and deep wooded valleys, becoming mountainous towards the north-east. The once-endangered red kite can often be seen soaring in Carmarthenshire skies.

CARMAR-THENSHIRE

Opposite Pendine Sands

Llanelli Beach

GRID REF **SS 495994**
GPS **51.6727°N, 4.1768°W**
COUNTY **Carmarthenshire**
BEACH FACES **South-west**

Llanelli has a small beach of coarse sand backed by a sea wall and low dunes, with stone breakwaters at either end. To the east are some smaller sandy coves. A pay & display car park is nearby, and facilities include a cafe, toilets and an ice cream shop. Cyclepaths run along the coast to Pembrey and inland along a former railway line to Cross Hands.

Signs warn against swimming. Other hazards include patches of mud and sandbanks which reach miles out into the bay.

Burry Port Beach

GRID REF **SN 447002**
GPS **51.6786°N, 4.2465°W**
COUNTY **Carmarthenshire**
BEACH FACES **South**

Once used for shipping coal from the nearby valleys, Burry Port's harbour is now a picturesque marina. To either side are sandy beaches, backed mostly by low dunes. Cyclepaths run along the coast eastwards to Llanelli and westwards to Pembrey. Plenty of pay & display car parks can be found at the harbour, and a small, free parking area is located at the end of Heol Vaughan (about 300 metres to the west).

Facilities include toilets, cycle parking, plenty of seating, a cafe and catering vans in summer. Signs warn against swimming and the danger of sandbanks. The village of Burry Port is a five-minute walk away and has a railway station (Pembrey & Burry Port), a supermarket, takeaways and pubs.

3 Pembrey Beach

Pembrey Beach (Cefn Sidan)

GRID REF **SS 400998**
GPS **51.6736°N, 4.3142°W**
COUNTY **Carmarthenshire**
BEACH FACES **South-west**

Llanelli

Swansea

Pembrey Beach stretches seven and a half miles from Burry Port harbour to Tywyn Point near Kidwelly. The shore is fine sand backed by dunes, behind which are the Saltings Nature Reserve, Pembrey Country Park, Pembrey Forest and RAF Pembrey. The beach has ten access points, each with information boards and numbered CE51 to CE60. Dog restrictions apply between points CE53 and CE57, stretching about three quarters of a mile, from May to September inclusive.

Space is plentiful on this beach but it's also very exposed, with little shelter from any wind. On a sunny day the sea warms quickly, but at low tide the sea can retreat almost a mile. Lifeguards patrol from the end of May until early September during weekends and school holidays only. Surf conditions can be good for an hour or two preceding the high tide. Rips are rare on the main part of the beach, but a strong high-tide cross-current often occurs.

Approximately one and a quarter miles west of the main beach access is a rock groyne built to deflect waves. The last access point (CE60) is another mile further west, and even on a hot day this part of the beach is often deserted. Pembrey Country Park's many facilities include a dry ski slope, a miniature railway, a visitor centre, cycle hire, an orienteering course, barbecue areas, woodland walks, an adventure playground and plenty of parking. Access to the beach from the car parks is a 200-metre walk, either over the dunes or on a tarmac road at the main beach access (CE56). Facilities here include toilets, a beach kiosk and seating area, drinking water and cold water showers.

Tywyn Point

GRID REF **SN 357065**
GPS **51.7326°N, 4.3795°W**
COUNTY **Carmarthenshire**
BEACH FACES **West**

Tywyn Point is at the extreme north-western end of Pembrey Sands, within the boundaries of the RAF zone of the beach, and so access is restricted usually to evenings and weekends. Wooden poles topped with orange tetrahedrons mark the boundaries, and red flags are flown from these when the firing range is in use, but otherwise this remote end of the beach is open.

At the north-western end of the beach is the Gwendraeth estuary and the wreck of the *Paul* which ran aground in October 1925.

Backed by low dunes, the sandy shore continues around the point finally ending at a salt marsh. There is no egress at this end, and swimming is dangerous due to currents. The nearest parking is at Pembrey Country Park – five miles away along the beach.

St Ishmaels

GRID REF **SN 362077**
GPS **51.7435°N, 4.3728°W**
COUNTY **Carmarthenshire**
BEACH FACES **West**

St Ishmaels lies about half a mile south of Ferryside. The shore is of shingle and some waste from iron smelters, backed by low dunes and the Swansea to Carmarthen railway. The Gwendraeth estuary is towards the south, where the shore becomes sandier and is backed by the Carmarthen Bay holiday village. Estuarine currents render swimming dangerous.

Limited parking can be found at the end of a track (signposted Old Parish Road) off the coast road, from where beach access is a short walk over a level crossing.

Ferryside

GRID REF **SN 365104**
GPS **51.7679°N, 4.3698°W**
COUNTY **Carmarthenshire**
BEACH FACES **West**

Ferryside lies on the east side of the Towy estuary opposite Llansteffan, and has a sandy beach backed by a sea wall and the Swansea to Carmarthen railway. A small parking area overlooks the shore and further parking is available in the village.

In the village you'll find toilets, a cafe, railway station, village stores and a pub. Signs warn against attempting to cross the estuary on foot and swimming. A passenger ferry now operates across the river to Llansteffan.

Llansteffan

GRID REF **SN 353104**
GPS **51.7675°N, 4.3872°W**
COUNTY **Carmarthenshire**
BEACH FACES **East**

Llansteffan, or Llanstephan, lies seven miles south of Carmarthen on the west side of the Towy estuary. The beach is mostly sand and cockle shells, backed by an area of rough grass, behind which are free car parking areas. Beach access is then down a short slipway. The sandy shore continues northwards for about a mile alongside the river, and southwards around the point to Scott's Bay. Signs warn against swimming and attempting to cross the estuary, and dog restrictions apply from 1 May to 30 September.

At the beach you'll find toilets, a small play area, fish & chip and ice cream vendors, and a tearoom/beach shop, and Llansteffan village is also a short walk away. A passenger ferry service operates across the Towy river to Ferryside. Overlooking the beach and village is the imposing free-to-enter Llansteffan Castle, which has panoramic views from its one accessible tower.

Scott's Bay

GRID REF **SN 347098**
GPS **51.7619°N, 4.3956°W**
COUNTY **Carmarthenshire**
BEACH FACES **South-east**

About half a mile south of Llansteffan, Scott's Bay is a sheltered, sandy bay backed by low cliffs of red sandstone and siltstone. Parking is available at Llansteffan and access to Scott's Bay is either by walking the coastal path or, tide permitting, along the shore. At low tide sandbars extend for over a mile out into Carmarthen Bay – swimming is dangerous at this time due to estuarial currents. To the south-west is Wharley Point, where the shore becomes rockier with patches of mud and some small caves.

About eighty metres behind the beach is St Anthony's Well – a place of pilgrimage for hundreds of years, hidden away in a tiny courtyard. Often adorned with shells and flowers, its waters are reputed to have healing properties. A plaque on the wall gives an insight into the well's history and another depicts St Anthony. To find it, follow the wide path heading inland and look for a door in the wall on the left.

2 **Ginst Point,** at the point looking towards Pembrey   3 **Ginst Point**   4 **Ginst Point,** the warning sign

Ginst Point (Laugharne Sands)

GRID REF **SN 325077**
GPS **51.7424°N, 4.4264°W**
COUNTY **Carmarthenshire**
BEACH FACES **South-east**

Ginst Point or Laugharne Sands (pronounced 'Larn', is at the far eastern end of Pendine Sands near the Taf estuary. The beach is fine sand with millions of shells, backed by low dunes and the Ministry of Defence firing range. Due to this access is limited, but the usual closure times are between 7 a.m. and 4 p.m. weekdays and some weekends. This is usually a very quiet beach as not many people know about it, but also very exposed with no shelter from the wind. Local dog walkers seem to be the main visitors. Signs warn against touching suspicious objects and swimming.

To get here, turn off the A4066 on the west side of Broadway village (signposted with hotel and B&B signs). Follow this straight road for a mile to the gates of the firing range, which are normally open after 4 p.m. Turn left and continue for a further two miles to the very end, where two small car parks can be seen on the left. Access to the beach is a sandy walk of about a hundred metres. The main beach is to the west and the sand continues all the way to Pendine. Not surprisingly, it's easy to find a long stretch completely deserted.

Pendine Sands

GRID REF **SN 234078**
GPS **51.7405°N, 4.5581°W**
COUNTY **Carmarthenshire**
BEACH FACES **South**

Pendine Sands is a six-and-a-quarter-mile beach reaching from Gilmore Point to Ginst Point. East of the village the shore is backed by dunes, with Ministry of Defence land behind. This area is off limits between 7 a.m. and 4 p.m. most days, although these times can vary. A red flag, a warning sign and a line of buoys mark the start of the restricted zone. Signs also warn of possible unexploded shells and prohibit the use of metal detectors. West of the village is

Dolwen Point, and a small bay of sand and rock pools backed by high limestone cliffs can be found on the other side. The coastal path can be accessed from here.

Parking is at a pay & display car park and, depending on the weather and tides, parking is also allowed on the sand from Easter to September. The beach is popular for jet skiing (club members only), kitesurfing and windsurfing. Access to the shore is down steps or one of the two slipways. The village has good facilities including toilets, pubs, a coffee shop, a restaurant, post office, beach shops, cafes and village stores. Lifeguards are on duty during the school summer holidays, and dog restrictions apply on a 100-metre section of the beach, between the Beach Hotel and the beach cafe, from 1 May to 30 September.

Morfa Bychan

GRID REF **SN 225074**
GPS **51.7367°N, 4.5709°W**
COUNTY **Carmarthenshire**
BEACH FACES **South**

Morfa Bychan is a small bay set in a steep-sided limestone valley between Ragwen and Gilman points. The sandy shore is backed by a storm bank of pebbles, behind which is a grassed area and some concrete relics of World War Two rehearsals.

There are four ways to get here:

1. Walk from Pendine along the shore at low tide.
2. Take the coastal path from Pendine which involves a steep ascent and descent.
3. Take the byway which leaves the Amroth road 140 metres west of the Green Bridge Inn. This is usually driveable, but very bumpy and sometimes muddy.
4. From Pendine drive to the top of the hill and park near the junction with the Amroth road. Take the bridleway on the west side of the road sixty metres south of the bus shelter. This leads downhill along a wooded valley. Keep to the left of the stream all the way.

Marros Sands

GRID REF **SN 206073**
GPS **51.7352°N, 4.5984°W**
COUNTY **Carmarthenshire**
BEACH FACES **South**

H'west • Narberth •

Tenby •

Whichever way you go, it's a long walk to get to Marros. The sandy beach is backed by a storm bank of pebbles and stretches about two miles from Telpyn Point at the western end to Ragwen Point. At low tide the patchy remains of a submerged forest can be seen and the wreck of a schooner, the *Rover*, which was beached during a gale in 1886, can be found at grid ref: SN 211072 (GPS: 51.7351°N, 4.5911°W). Towards the western end there are cliffs and caves.

It never gets busy here, but being remote it has become popular with local naturists.

Some roadside parking can be found at Marros village and access is along a public footpath which runs from St Lawrence's church to the coastal path, thence continuing down to the shore. The horizontal distance is about a mile, and the church is 136 metres above sea level. If the tide is low, walking along the shore from Amroth or Telpyn beaches is an easier option. Alternatively, roadside parking about half a mile east of Amroth, found at grid ref: SN 181076 (GPS: 51.7375°N, 4.6357°W), gives access to the coastal path. After approximately three quarters of a mile, the path descends into a secluded, steep-sided valley providing access to the western end of Marros.

Telpyn Beach

GRID REF **SN 183072**
GPS **51.7335°N, 4.6316°W**
COUNTY **Carmarthenshire**
BEACH FACES **South**

Telpyn Beach lies west of Telpyn Point, at the Carmarthenshire end of Amroth Beach. It's a wide, sandy beach backed by a pebble bank and unstable cliffs. A wave-cut platform at the point is a popular area for sunbathing, and at low tide it's possible to walk around the point to Marros. Swimming is generally safe.

Roadside parking is available about half a mile east of Amroth at grid ref: SN 181076 (GPS: 51.7375°N, 4.6357°W), from where a public footpath leads to the coastal path, which then continues down to the shore. Alternatively, walking along the shore from Amroth is possible between low and mid tide.

Pembrokeshire is home to Britain's only coastal national park and some of the finest beaches in South Wales. The main resort beaches are Saundersfoot and Tenby in the south-east – both accessible by rail (although a bit of a walk for Saundersfoot). The south-western tip of Pembrokeshire has spectacular small bays backed by high limestone cliffs, which are popular with climbers. Along the west coast, surf beaches can be found at Freshwater West, Newgale and Whitesands. Pembrokeshire's north coast is indented with quieter, sandy beaches and secret coves. The county's highest point is Foel Cwmcerwyn in the Preseli Hills, at 536 metres. Lifeguards patrol the main beaches in summer, and boat trips operate to the islands of Caldey, Skomer and Ramsey.

PEM-BROKE-SHIRE

Opposite Skrinkle Haven

Amroth

GRID REF **SN 164069**
GPS **51.7302°N, 4.6589°W**
COUNTY **Pembrokeshire**
BEACH FACES **South**

H'west
Narberth
Tenby

The village of Amroth lies on the border of Pembrokeshire and Carmarthenshire, the stream at the eastern side of the village being the county boundary. Backed by a storm bank of pebbles and a sea wall, its sandy beach is generally safe for swimming and watersports, and the neighbouring beaches of Wisemans Bridge, Telpyn and Marros can be reached along the shore at low tide. Amroth often suffers during winter storms; at one time there were houses on both sides of the road.

Free parking is available on the pebbly roadside verge at the eastern end, or at one of two small car parks. Access to the shore is down a slipway or a short walk across the pebble bank. Lifeguards patrol during July and August, and dog restrictions apply on the central section of the beach from 1 May to 30 September. Facilities include toilets at both ends of the beach, two pubs, a cafe and beach shop.

Wisemans Bridge

GRID REF **SN 145060**
GPS **51.7215°N, 4.6859°W**
COUNTY **Pembrokeshire**
BEACH FACES **South-east**

The hamlet of Wisemans Bridge has a beach of rocks, sand and shingle, with a substantial stream, Fords Lake, emerging on the southern side. The shore northwards is initially rocky, becoming increasingly sandy on the approach to Amroth. To the south it's a mix of rocks, sand and rock pools, with a freshwater spring issuing on to the beach just before Coppet Hall Point.

Facilities include toilets and a pub, Wisemans Bridge Inn, with outdoor seating. Free parking is available on the pebbly verge overlooking the beach.

Coppet Hall

GRID REF **SN 141054**
GPS **51.7160°N, 4.6914°W**
COUNTY **Pembrokeshire**
BEACH FACES **East**

At the northern end of Saundersfoot Bay, Coppet Hall is a sandy beach backed by some shingle and a pay & display car park. Facilities include toilets and a Beach Centre with a bar/restaurant. A voluntary dog ban operates between 10 a.m. and 5 p.m. from 1 May to 30 September. Saundersfoot Railway Station is just over a mile away, and Coppet Hall can be reached by following the B4316 down to St Issells church and taking a public footpath through the Old Mill Caravan Park.

The name 'Coppet Hall' is believed to derive from 'Coal Pit Haul', a reference to its earlier mining days. A former colliery tramway which ran from Saundersfoot harbour to Stepaside is now a foot/cyclepath, linking Coppet Hall to Saundersfoot through a seventy-metre tunnel, and to Wisemans Bridge via tunnels of twenty and 100 metres. Two old mine adits, which are now blocked off, can be seen adjacent to the path.

Saundersfoot

GRID REF **SN 137048**
GPS **51.7104°N, 4.6969°W**
COUNTY **Pembrokeshire**
BEACH FACES **East**

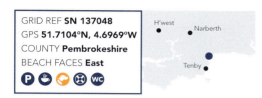

Saundersfoot is one of Pembrokeshire's more popular beaches, and can get busy, especially at high tide. A pay & display car park at the harbour overlooks the sandy shore, and additional parking is available a short distance away. Beach access is down a slipway.

Facilities include pubs, cafes, beach shops and toilets. Fishing trips operate in summer and drinking water is available from taps along the southern harbour wall. Lifeguards patrol

from late June until early September, and dog restrictions apply from the harbour northwards for approximately 350 metres from 1 May to 30 September – the alleyway to The Strand being the northern boundary.

Originally built to export anthracite from local pits, the harbour was served by a narrow-gauge railway with two branches. One branch ran directly inland, and its route can be followed via Brookland Place, the Incline and Fan Road to Saundersfoot's railway station about one and a quarter miles away. The second branch ran along The Strand, passing through tunnels to Coppet Hall and Wisemans Bridge. This route is now a foot/cyclepath.

The beach looks out across Carmarthen Bay to Rhossili Down and Worm's Head on the Gower Peninsula.

Glen Beach & Swallow Tree

Glen Beach

GRID REF **SN 138045**
GPS **51.7078°N, 4.6953°W**
COUNTY **Pembrokeshire**
BEACH FACES **East**

H'west
Narberth
Tenby

Glen Beach lies south of the harbour at Saundersfoot, consisting of sand, rocks, small streams and rock pools, backed by cliffs of mudstone and sandstone. Opposite the harbour is a classic example of an anticline known as Ladies' Cave, beyond which are some small, sandy coves backed by wooded cliffs. The first of these is St Brides Bay. The next

along has a mine adit at the back corner, and the third, Swallow Tree, gives easy access to the coastal path and is popular for fishing and high-tide swimming. As these beaches face east, the upper shore becomes shaded towards late afternoon. Around low tide it's possible to walk to Monkstone Point , which you can see in the distance below, and Monkstone Beach.

Access from Saundersfoot harbour is down an easy ramp. Alternatively, at the bottom of The Glen, the first turning on the left after St Brides hill out of Saundersfoot, roadside parking for about fifteen cars is available, and beach access is a short concrete path with steps. Toilets and drinking water are available at Saundersfoot harbour.

Monkstone Beach

GRID REF: **SN 146031**
GPS **51.6955°N, 4.6830°W**
COUNTY **Pembrokeshire**
BEACH FACES **South-east**

Approximately halfway between Saundersfoot and Tenby, Monkstone Beach consists of fine sand backed by a storm bank of pebbles, and high, unstable cliffs of shale and sandstone. At high tide most of the sand is covered, but this sheltered bay provides generally safe conditions for swimming, while the rocks near the headland are popular for diving and jumping.

The southern end of the beach becomes accessible at low to mid tide, and is rockier, with streams, rock pools and a waterfall. Access to the coastal path is possible here by walking up a steep rock slab. Only on exceptionally low tides is it possible to proceed further along the shore towards Tenby. In the opposite direction, Saundersfoot can be reached along the shore at low tide – the critical cut-off point being just the other side of the headland.

Roadside parking is available on the lane to Trevayne Farm Camping & Caravan Park, from where a permissive path continues through the farm to the coastal path. A well-maintained, steep path with nearly 200 steps descends the wooded cliffs to the beach. Another path leads out to the headland, from where it's possible to scramble with some difficulty down to the beach.

1 Waterwynch, cove north of Waterwynch   **2** Waterwynch, inside one of the caves   **3** Waterwynch Bay

Waterwynch Bay

GRID REF **SN 137019**
GPS **51.6844°N, 4.6953°W**
COUNTY **Pembrokeshire**
BEACH FACES **East**

Waterwynch is a small bay about three quarters of a mile north of Tenby. Access is a walk of about half a mile along a public footpath from the A478 just south of New Hedges. Parking for a maximum of two cars is possible at this end of the lane, but as Waterwynch is a small, quiet beach there is usually space here. Alternative access is from Tenby via the coastal path.

The beach is sand with a pebble bank and a small stream running down the north side. Waterwynch House sits in the narrow valley directly behind the beach; the upper part of the shore (above the mean high tide mark) is owned by that estate. On either side of Waterwynch further small coves can be reached at low tide. Those to the north are best, and boast some impressive caves.

Usually there is only one way on and off Waterwynch beach; there is no access to the coastal path from any of the coves on either side, and walking to the neighbouring beaches of Monkstone or Tenby is only possible on exceptionally low tides.

Tenby North & Tenby Harbour

Tenby North

GRID REF **SN 133007**
GPS **51.6735°N, 4.7005°W**
COUNTY **Pembrokeshire**
BEACH FACES **East**

H'west · Narberth

Tenby

Tenby's North Beach is a wide, sandy bay backed by a sea wall and high cliffs. Goscar Rock sits at the centre of the beach, and towards the southern end is Tenby's picturesque harbour, which has its own sheltered, sandy beach. The road known as The Croft runs along the clifftop, and from it a zigzag path provides beach access for anything with wheels.

The cliffs provide good shelter for sunbathing, and it's generally safe for swimming. Toilets and drinking water are available at the back of the beach.

Some roadside parking can be found on The Croft, but spaces here are quickly taken. Tenby's large pay & display North Beach car park is located off the A478 and connected to The Croft via a walkway, with a long flight of steps to North Beach.

Lifeguards patrol from late June until early September and a dog ban applies to North Beach and Harbour from 1 May to 30 September. Tenby has good facilities, including a Tourist Information Centre, pubs, cafes, hotels, shops, a supermarket and a railway station.

1 Tenby Castle Beach, with South Beach in distance   **2** Tenby South Beach   **3** Penally Beach

Tenby Castle Beach

GRID REF **SN 137003**
GPS **51.6700°N, 4.6945°W**
COUNTY **Pembrokeshire**
BEACH FACES **South-east**

Tenby's Castle Beach lies at the eastern end of the town between the North and South beaches. There are no car parks nearby and access is through the town and down a slipway or, tide permitting, along the shore from South Beach.

The shore is sandy, backed by limestone cliffs and overlooked by hotels. On the north side, the sea deepens quickly and boat trips to Caldey Island (see page 329) depart from here. Facilities include toilets and a cafe on the slipway, while the cafes, pubs and shops of Tenby are only a short walk away. Lifeguards patrol from late June until early September and dog restrictions apply from 1 May to 30 September.

St Catherine's Island is privately owned and has some walk-through caves which can be explored on a low tide.

Tenby South & Penally Beach

Tenby South

GRID REF **SN 132000**
GPS **51.6672°N, 4.7015°W**
COUNTY **Pembrokeshire**
BEACH FACES **East**

Tenby's South Beach stretches about a mile from the town to Giltar Point and looks out towards Caldey Island, which is about two miles offshore. The shore is of sand and some pebbles, backed by dunes covered in sea buckthorn. Being east facing, offshore winds occur frequently, so inflatable crafts should be used with caution.

A pay & display car park is located behind the beach and access to the shore is a short walk over the sand. Facilities include toilets, drinking water and a bar/restaurant. Dogs are not allowed north of the beach access point from 1 May to 30 September but are allowed to the south. Lifeguards patrol from late May until early September, as well as on weekends from Easter.

The beach's southern end is known as Penally Beach, and is a short, level walk along a tarmac footpath from Penally Railway Station. It's a good beach for seashells and generally safe for swimming, but a strong rip current occurs near Giltar Point.

Lydstep Haven

GRID REF **SS 092982**
GPS **51.6497°N, 4.7583°W**
COUNTY **Pembrokeshire**
BEACH FACES **East**

Lydstep Haven beach is about half a mile long and dominated by the private holiday park behind it. A beach of sand and pebbles, flanked by limestone cliffs and backed with a sea defence wall of rocks, it looks out towards Sandtop Bay on Caldey Island.

Access is down a steep slipway, and nearby facilities include toilets, drinking water and a small shop. In summer, the northern half of the beach has a designated swimming zone and a dog ban operates on this section from 1 May to 30 September. Parking for non-residents is at a free National Trust car park at Lydstep Head. This can be reached by turning off the A4139 at Lydstep village on to a byway signposted as a no through road. After approximately 300 metres along this track, a turning on the right leads to the car park at the top of the hill.

Lydstep Caverns

GRID REF **SS 086975**
GPS **51.6441°N, 4.7666°W**
COUNTY **Pembrokeshire**
BEACH FACES **South**

Tenby

Lydstep Caverns is a sandy beach located west of Lydstep Head. Visiting on anything other than a low tide may bring disappointment, however, as most of the beach will be underwater. The high limestone cliffs which back it mean it is a popular venue for climbers. As its name suggests, it has some spectacular caves and arches and is a good beach for fossil collecting.

Parking is either at Skrinkle Haven or the closer Lydstep Head (see previous beach). From here, follow the coastal path westwards to the bottom of the valley, where a rough path leads on to the rocks at the back of the beach.

Church Doors & Skrinkle Haven

Church Doors

GRID REF **SS 080974**
GPS **51.6421°N, 4.7752°W**
COUNTY **Pembrokeshire**
BEACH FACES **South-east**

Church Doors and Skrinkle Haven are two neighbouring coves separated by a narrow headland, and are best visited around low tide. Church Doors is a small rocky cove with some low-tide sand. Skrinkle Haven is mostly sandy and is backed by high cliffs of limestone, changing to Old Red sandstone on the west side.

A free car park is located on the clifftop adjacent to the coastal path. It can be reached by turning off the B4585 (Manorbier Road) in Skrinkle village and continuing past the artillery range and youth hostel to the very end of the road. From here follow the coastal path westwards for about 300 metres. Access to Church Doors is down steep concrete steps, which lead to a metal stairway, with 140 steps in total. The high rock arch which gives the cove its name is directly in front.

Skrinkle Haven can then be reached by walking around the headland, or by a narrow, slippery cave which pierces the headland and ends at a rock pool. Both means of access and egress are tide dependent. Dogs are allowed at all times, but may need to be carried on the metal stairway which has open tread steps.

Presipe Bay

GRID REF **SS 069970**
GPS **51.6381°N, 4.7909°W**
COUNTY **Pembrokeshire**
BEACH FACES **South**

Presipe Bay (pronounced 'Prez-ippee') is one of Pembrokeshire's secret beaches, and is best visited within two hours of low tide: at other times it's mostly underwater. The shore is sandy, surrounded by cliffs of sandstone and mudstone in almost vertical strata. It can be good for surfing around low tide once the sea is clear of the rocks. Access is from the coastal path, with 162 steep steps descending to the shore.

To get there, turn off the B4585 (Manorbier Road) in Skrinkle village towards the youth hostel and take the coastal path on the right immediately before the artillery range. Roadside parking is possible here. Follow the path around the perimeter of the range and across a field to reach the steps at the west side of the beach. Alternative access is via the coastal path from Manorbier.

Manorbier

GRID REF **SS 060975**
GPS **51.6423°N, 4.8041°W**
COUNTY **Pembrokeshire**
BEACH FACES **South-west**

Overlooked by a twelfth-century castle, a small stream crosses the shore of Manorbier Beach, which consists of coarse sand and pebbles flanked by red sandstone cliffs.

This is a popular surfing beach, best visited an hour or two after high tide, but surfers often have to compete for space with body-boarders, canoeists and the occasional angler.

The pay & display car park is located in the valley behind the beach, and has toilets and usually an ice cream van in summer.

Beach access is along a gravelled path. Some free roadside parking overlooking the bay can be found a little further along the lane, often used by surfers. Adjacent to the coastal path on the eastern side of the bay is the cromlech of King's Quoit. There are deep zawns close to the path here, one of which emerges on the landward side of the path and is unfenced.

Manorbier village is a short walk away and has a tearoom, pub, and a shop. Manorbier Railway Station is about one and a quarter miles from the beach.

2 Swanlake Bay   **3** Swanlake Bay, tideline   **4** Swanlake Bay, from the west

Swanlake Bay

GRID REF **SS 046980**
GPS **51.6463°N, 4.8246°W**
COUNTY **Pembrokeshire**
BEACH FACES **South-west**

Swanlake Bay is a remote sandy beach about a mile west of Manorbier. Access is by footpath from Freshwater East or Manorbier, or the public footpath running from West Moor Farm. From Manorbier Beach it is possible to take the coastal path, but a quicker and easier route is to follow the lane to the top of the hill, where there are some parking spaces, and take the footpath on the left.

The sand on the shore is coarse and gravelly, and at low tide the beach extends to the west, becoming 650 metres wide. This part of the shore consists of red sandstone rocks, which are jagged and difficult to walk over, and some low-tide sand. The beach has excellent water quality, but there can be rip currents in surf conditions, particularly on the east side. Being somewhat remote, it has become popular with local naturists.

Freshwater East

GRID REF **SS 018975**
GPS **51.6408°N, 4.8648°W**
COUNTY **Pembrokeshire**
BEACH FACES **East**

Freshwater East is a popular sandy bay flanked by cliffs of mudstone and sandstone. Although there are no lifeguards, it's generally safe for swimming, windsurfing and kayaking. Parking is at a pay & display car park, from which a level walk of about 200 metres leads to the beach. Facilities include toilets, a slipway on to the sand and usually an ice cream van in the car park. Offshore winds frequently occur, so inflatable crafts should be used with caution.

Stackpole Quay

GRID REF **SR 994958**
GPS **51.6247°N, 4.8984°W**
COUNTY **Pembrokeshire**
BEACH FACES **East**

Stackpole Quay is a small but picturesque harbour on the National Trust's Stackpole Estate. Originally built to serve local limestone quarries, it's now a popular venue for kayaking. There is some sand at low tide, but very little beach available at high tide. The harbour area can be accessed via a metal ladder during this time. A National Trust car park is set in the valley behind the beach, and facilities include toilets and tearooms.

3 Barafundle Bay   4 Barafundle Bay, from the woods southside   5 Barafundle Bay, Lort's Cave

Barafundle Bay

GRID REF **SR 991950**
GPS **51.6174°N, 4.9023°W**
COUNTY **Pembrokeshire**
BEACH FACES **East**

Barafundle Bay lies within the National Trust's Stackpole Estate, and is often regarded as Pembrokeshire's best beach. Approximately 300 metres wide, the sandy shore is backed by low dunes and flanked by limestone cliffs. It's very sheltered, making it good for sunbathing and swimming.

On low spring tides caves and arches on the north side can be explored. Lort's Cave is one of the larger ones, and nearby a low cave leads to a secret beach. Spring tides in Pembrokeshire occur when the low tide time is around 2 or 3 p.m. The closest parking is at an attended National Trust car park at Stackpole Quay, from where access to Barafundle is a mostly level walk of half a mile along the coastal path.

There are no facilities at the beach, but Stackpole Quay has toilets and tearooms. Behind the beach and dunes a path follows the valley through woodland, eventually reaching a track which can then be followed back to the car park at Stackpole Quay. Although this is not usually a surf beach, conditions can be good with a big swell and a northerly wind.

Mowingword Bay

GRID REF **SR 990943**
GPS **51.6111°N, 4.9033°W**
COUNTY **Pembrokeshire**
BEACH FACES **South**

Mowingword Bay is a beach of superlatives. Lying on the opposite side of Stackpole Head from Barafundle Bay, it easily surpasses this as Pembrokeshire's best beach. The shore is of sand, rocks and rock pools, and there are also some cathedral-like walk-through caves – including one with a blowhole reaching to the top of the cliffs.

At the centre of the bay is Pinnacle Stack, while the headland of Mowingword on the eastern side is a popular climbing spot. Unfortunately it's also the most difficult beach to get to. Access is at low tide by paddleboard or kayak from Broad Haven South, or alternatively by a 400-metre swim from neighbouring Box Bay – another beach with difficult access. Approximately halfway is the narrow, sandy inlet of Raming Hole. Even in the height of summer, you're likely to have the beach all to yourself, as seen in this photo, which was taken at low tide. Parking is at Broad Haven South.

3 Box Bay, from the east, showing the easiest way down   **4** Box Bay   **5** Box Bay, the route down

Box Bay

GRID REF **SR 983942**
GPS **51.6099°N, 4.9134°W**
COUNTY **Pembrokeshire**
BEACH FACES **South-east**

The picturesque sandy cove of Box Bay lies just east of Broad Haven South beach. Surrounded by high limestone cliffs, access is difficult and you should not attempt to visit this beach unless you are confident of your ability to reach and leave it safely. There are a few possible ways on to the shore, the best of which is a

ten-metre climb down the rocks on the west side. You need to be reasonably proficient at climbing, and a rope would certainly be advisable, but specialist climbing skills or equipment are not necessary. A rusty belay stake has been fixed into the rocks just before the steepest section, and the route is indicated in the photo below. Bear in mind this needs to be done around low tide.

Behind the beach is a sinkhole known as Sandy Pit, which connects to the beach via a small cave. Depending on what the winter storms have done this is sometimes passable, but more often than not completely blocked. The nearest parking is at Broad Haven South.

Broad Haven South

GRID REF **SR 977939**
GPS **51.6070°N, 4.9219°W**
COUNTY **Pembrokeshire**
BEACH FACES **South-east**

Set in spectacular limestone scenery between the headland of Saddle Point and Star Rock, Broad Haven South is a wide, sandy beach backed by dunes. A stream from the Bosherston lily ponds flows along the eastern side, usually creating a large pool ideal for splashing around in, while an effusive freshwater spring can be found on the opposite side near Star Rock. Just out to sea is the limestone stack of Church Rock.

Behind the dunes are two valleys: the more easterly of the two leads to the Bosherston lily ponds, while the other, Mere Pool Valley, has a track leading back to the car park access road. Parking is at a National Trust pay & display car park. The car park is listed as a Dark Sky Discovery Site: a place largely free from light pollution, suitable for stargazing.

Access to the shore is a concrete path with steps which leads about two-thirds of the way down, the remainder being a descent of the dunes. Getting anything with wheels on to the beach is difficult, and getting it off again even more so. Facilities include toilets, drinking water and showers. Bosherston village is about a mile away, and has tearooms, a pub and a good-size car park, from where footpaths lead to the beach via the lily ponds.

Trevallen Coves

GRID REF **SR 976935**
GPS **51.6034°N, 4.9231°W**
COUNTY **Pembrokeshire**
BEACH FACES **East**

Trevallen Coves are two sandy beaches connected by a low-tide cave through a narrow headland. The north cove is accessible at all times but the south cove, known locally as Little Horn, lies inside the Ministry of Defence Castlemartin Range and is therefore subject to access restrictions. Access to either involves negotiating a steep path and rocks.

The southern end of the National Trust car park for Broad Haven South is just 100 metres away, and facilities include toilets, drinking water and usually a refreshment van.

New Quay

GRID REF **SR 974931**
GPS **51.5997°N, 4.9257°W**
COUNTY **Pembrokeshire**
BEACH FACES **East**

Situated within the Ministry of Defence's Castlemartin Range, New Quay is a narrow, sandy inlet surrounded by limestone cliffs. Access is restricted usually to evenings and weekends. To get there you need to park in the Range car park at St Govan's Head and take the coastal path heading east until you see the head of a narrow valley. This can be followed down to the beach. Alternatively, park at the National Trust car park for Broad Haven South and take the coastal path westwards.

A recorded message giving precise firing times for the Castlemartin Range is available on 01646 662367.

Bullslaughter Bay

GRID REF **SR 941942**
GPS **51.6084°N, 4.9740°W**
COUNTY **Pembrokeshire**
BEACH FACES **South**

Lying within the Ministry of Defence's Castlemartin Range, access to Bullslaughter Bay is restricted usually to evenings and weekends. The free Range car park at Elegug Stacks has picnic tables, cycle stands and an emergency telephone. Bullslaughter Bay is about a mile to the east and access is a walk or cycle along the

coastal path, this section of which is a bridleway, followed by a steep descent down a grassy gully on the beach's eastern side.

Clean, golden sand makes up the shore, with small streams and rock pools. At the back of the beach are some impressive caves and arches, and the beach is good for sunbathing, photography, angling and climbing. Swimming is generally safe close inshore.

A recorded message giving precise firing times for the Castlemartin Range is available on 01646 662367.

Flimston Bay

GRID REF **SR 931946**
GPS **51.6116°N, 4.9886°W**
COUNTY **Pembrokeshire**
BEACH FACES **South**

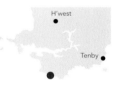

Flimston Bay is a picturesque beach in the Castlemartin Ministry of Defence Range, meaning access is usually restricted to evenings and weekends. About 180 metres wide, it consists of sand backed by shingle and high

limestone cliffs. Free parking is available at the Range car park at Elegug Stacks. From here Flimston Bay is approximately 500 metres east along the coastal path. Access to the shore involves a tricky scramble down a steep gully in the cliffs at the north-west corner – there is often a rope here, but it is possible to get down unaided. This beach is probably best avoided in wet conditions and it's no place to bring your granny, young children or dogs.

A recorded message giving precise firing times for the Castlemartin Range is available on 01646 662367.

Pen-y-holt Bay

GRID REF **SR 895955**
GPS **51.6184°N, 5.0411°W**
COUNTY **Pembrokeshire**
BEACH FACES **South**

Pen-y-holt Bay lies within the Ministry of Defence's Castlemartin Range, and is **off limits to the general public at all times**. It's a beach of rocks and some small amounts of low-tide sand, backed by high limestone cliffs.

Hobbyhorse Bay

GRID REF **SR 886957**
GPS **51.6198°N, 5.0542°W**
COUNTY **Pembrokeshire**
BEACH FACES **South**

Within the Ministry of Defence's Castlemartin Range, Hobbyhorse Bay is **off limits to the general public at all times**. It lies a quarter of a mile east of Linney Head, and is a small bay of sand, rocks and a sea stack said to resemble a hobbyhorse. The bay is often used by seals for breeding and at low tide Crow Rock can be seen about half a mile offshore.

Blucks Pool

GRID REF **SR 889972**
GPS **51.6334°N, 5.0508°W**
COUNTY **Pembrokeshire**
BEACH FACES **West**

Lying to the south of the rocky headland of The Pole, Blucks Pool is a secluded, funnel-shaped cove situated within the Castlemartin Ministry of Defence Range. About 150 metres wide, and backed by Linney Burrows, it's **off limits to the general public at all times**.

Frainslake Sands

GRID REF **SR 889980**
GPS **51.6406°N, 5.0512°W**
COUNTY **Pembrokeshire**
BEACH FACES **West**

Frainslake Sands is in the Castlemartin Ministry of Defence Range and lies between the headland of Great Furzenip and the smaller rocky headland of The Pole. Approximately two thirds of a mile wide and backed by Brownslade Burrows, the shore is comprised of coarse sand with a few rocky outcrops. Although it's **off limits to the general public at all times**, genuine surfers and anglers can now obtain permits by attending a safety briefing at Merrion Camp.

The beach gets its name from the stream of Frains Lake, which flows over the shingle at the southern end ('lake' is Pembrokeshire dialect for a stream or river). Organised walks on the Castlemartin Range take place in spring and summer, details of which are available from Tourist Information Centres.

Freshwater West

GRID REF **SR 884997**
GPS **51.6557°N, 5.0595°W**
COUNTY **Pembrokeshire**
BEACH FACES **West**

H'west

Tenby

Known locally as 'Fresh West', this is one of Pembrokeshire's most popular surf beaches, with the surf consistent at most stages of the tide. Signs warn against swimming as strong rip currents are common and can occur anywhere on the beach. Places to be particularly careful are near the reef, and towards the northern end. The shore is golden sand backed by dunes and the water quality is usually excellent.

There are two free car parking areas: the main car park and roadside parking are at the southern end, while a smaller car park can accommodate approximately twenty cars at the northern end. Depending on which car park you use, beach access is either a short walk down a concrete footpath on to the shingle or a 200-metre walk across the dunes. Facilities include toilets and usually a van serving refreshments. Lifeguards patrol from the end of June until early September.

West Angle Bay

GRID REF **SM 853032**
GPS **51.6859°N, 5.1064°W**
COUNTY **Pembrokeshire**
BEACH FACES **West**

West Angle Bay lies at the western end of the Castlemartin peninsula, a mile west of Angle village. A free car park is located behind the beach, and facilities include toilets, a cafe and cycle stands. Access is down a gentle ramp.

The sandy beach is flanked by cliffs of shale and limestone, with plenty of fossils to be found. A popular beach, it's generally good for swimming and sunbathing, and halfway along the north side is a hidden beach which can be reached from the coastal path.

Angle Bay

GRID REF **SM 897021**
GPS **51.6777°N, 5.0422°W**
COUNTY **Pembrokeshire**
BEACH FACES **North**

Angle Bay lies on the southern side of Milford Haven, and is a wide bay of sandstone rocks, shingle, seaweed and plenty of mud. The eastern side has some small patches of sand and a parking area at grid ref: SM 897020 (GPS 51.6776°N, 5.0415°W). Parking on the west side is at Old Point House pub in Angle village – a track beginning at the church leads alongside the bay to the parking area.

Bullwell Bay

GRID REF **SM 901039**
GPS **51.6940°N, 5.0375°W**
COUNTY **Pembrokeshire**
BEACH FACES **North**

At first glance, Bullwell Bay would appear to be an uninteresting place. Located directly opposite the town of Milford Haven, it's a small beach with jetties serving the oil tankers a few hundred metres offshore. The beach is backed by wooded slopes, a ruined farmhouse and an old lime kiln. However, a visitor to the shore will find millions of shells here: limpets, mussels, saddle oysters, tower shells, winkles, European cowries and more are likely finds. Pieces of sea-glass are also quite abundant.

The nearest parking space is at Angle Bay. From here, the coastal path follows a private road towards Popton Fort. Final access to the shore is down one of two paths, the one on the east side being the easiest.

Gelliswick Bay

GRID REF **SM 886055**
GPS **51.7092°N, 5.0601°W**
COUNTY **Pembrokeshire**
BEACH FACES **South**

Gelliswick Bay is on the north side of the Milford Haven waterway, and the beach of pebbles and weed-strewn sand is backed by a sea wall. On the east side is Fort Hubberston, which has no public access, and behind the beach is a grass area. Roadside parking is available, and access to the shore is down a slipway.

Kilroom

GRID REF **SM 868059**
GPS **51.7107°N, 5.0864°W**
COUNTY **Pembrokeshire**
BEACH FACES **West**

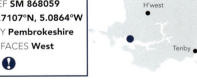

Kilroom is a little-known beach of sandstone rocks, rock pools and sand, situated north of South Hook Point. It's very sheltered, making it suited to sunbathing, and a further sandy cove to the west is accessible at low tide.

Access from the coastal path is a steep, rugged path following a stream, so although dogs are allowed access may prove difficult. The closest parking is at Sandy Haven. Alternatively, park in Herbrandston village and follow the narrow lane south, taking a footpath on the right ninety metres after the Sandy Haven turning. This leads to the coastal path at the east side of Sandy Haven Beach, from where Kilroom is three quarters of a mile eastwards.

1 Sandy Haven **2** Sleeping Bay **3** Longoar Bay, a calm day **4** Longoar Bay, from the coastal path

Sandy Haven

GRID REF **SM 857072**
GPS **51.7220°N, 5.1031°W**
COUNTY **Pembrokeshire**
BEACH FACES **South**

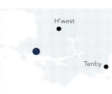

A lane leads from the village of Herbrandston to a free car park overlooking Sandy Haven. The shore is a mix of sand, rocks and rock pools, but the top of the beach will mostly be covered in a high tide.

Access to the shore is a short walk over the rocks or down a flight of steps 140 metres east of the car park. The narrow lane continues to a slipway on to Sandy Haven Pill, which has a small stream. Although the coastal path crosses this, the crossing can only be used for approximately three hours either side of low tide. At other times it's a four-mile detour along roads to reach the other side. Swimming is generally safe and rocks provide plenty of sheltered areas for sunbathing.

Sleeping Bay

GRID REF **SM 855068**
GPS **51.7183°N, 5.1057°W**
COUNTY **Pembrokeshire**
BEACH FACES **South-east**

Sleeping Bay is a small cove of red sandstone rocks and seaweed-strewn sand. Access is from the western side of Sandy Haven by wading across the Sandy Haven Pill during the low-tide period. This is the only route on and off the beach, so take care not to get cut off by the incoming tide. There are low cliffs around the beach, which in several places can be easily climbed, although a wide margin of dense thorny scrub separates the clifftop from the coastal path.

Longoar Bay

GRID REF **SM 849061**
GPS **51.7118°N, 5.1140°W**
COUNTY **Pembrokeshire**
BEACH FACES **East**

Longoar Bay is a remote beach on the eastern side of Great Castle Head. The sandy shore has many rocks and rock pools and is bordered by sandstone cliffs. A bridleway leads northwards from Great Castle Head across fields to meet Sandy Haven at St Ishmaels road, grid ref: SM 846072 (GPS: 51.7221°N, 5.1196°W). This has plenty of space for roadside parking.

Access to the shore is tricky; the only route down is a steep, rugged path at the approximate centre of the bay, which leads on to the rocks at the back of the beach. A narrow gap in the blackthorn bushes reveals its location.

Lindsway Bay & Wenall Bay

Lindsway Bay

GRID REF **SM 843066**
GPS **51.7161°N, 5.1229°W**
COUNTY **Pembrokeshire**
BEACH FACES **South-west**

St Davids

H'west

Tenby

Lying between Rook's Nest Point and Longberry Point, Lindsway Bay is a small sandy cove on the north side of the Milford Haven Waterway. The nearest parking is by the playing fields at St Ishmaels, from where an asphalt footpath leads alongside the sports pitches to the coastal path. A stone seat at the path junction offers panoramic views of the Milford Haven Waterway. About 350 metres east of this, access to Lindsway Bay is down a steep zigzag path with 108 steps, followed by a short walk over the sandstone boulders.

West of the main beach a similar but smaller cove is accessible for about one and a half hours either side of low tide. Wenall Bay is the next cove and has a shore of pebbles, streams, rock pools and some sand. It can only be reached around the point when the tide is at its lowest, but even then this will involve some scrambling over the rocks. Be aware of the state of the tide if visiting this beach.

Monk Haven

GRID REF **SM 828063**
GPS **51.7128°N, 5.1444°W**
COUNTY **Pembrokeshire**
BEACH FACES **South**

H'west

Tenby

Monk Haven is a narrow, sheltered cove of red sandstone pebbles and some low-tide sand near the village of St Ishmaels. It's backed by a high castellated wall and flanked by low cliffs of red sandstone. The wall was built in the eighteenth century to mark the boundary of the Trewarren Estate and the remains of a tower can be seen adjacent to the coastal path to the east.

Access is via the coastal path or by taking a narrow lane (signposted to Monk Haven) on the west side of St Ishmaels village. This leads to St Ishmaels church, where there is very limited space for parking. From here, a good footpath continues along the wooded valley to the beach.

The Gann Beach

GRID REF **SM 809066**
GPS **51.7148°N, 5.1721°W**
COUNTY **Pembrokeshire**
BEACH FACES **East**
Ⓟ

The Gann Beach is a long shingle ridge north of Dale backed by a wall of boulders, behind which are tidal lagoons. The upper shore consists of small sandstone pebbles, shells and some sand, and the lower shore of seaweed-strewn sand and rocks.

The coastal path runs behind the beach and crosses the River Gann by a tidal bridge, which can be used for about three and a half hours either side of low tide. A small, roadside parking area alongside the B4327 overlooks the shore and has views towards Milford Haven Waterway.

Dale

GRID REF **SM 812058**
GPS **51.7077°N, 5.1672°W**
COUNTY **Pembrokeshire**
BEACH FACES **East**
Ⓟ 🏖 🔵 ⓌⒸ

Dale is on the north side of the Milford Haven Waterway at the end of the B4327. Not exactly a beach for paddling and sandcastles, the shore is full of sand and stones, and the sea is cluttered with assorted buoys. However, being east facing and sheltered means it's better for windsurfing and sailing.

Dog restrictions apply on the northern section of the beach from May to September inclusive, and parking is at a small, landscaped pay & display car park. Dale has good facilities, which include toilets, a slipway, a cafe, pub and restaurant. The village also has a tediously long one-way system.

Castlebeach Bay

GRID REF **SM 820049**
GPS **51.6999°N, 5.1551°W**
COUNTY **Pembrokeshire**
BEACH FACES **East**

Castlebeach is a small bay of red sandstone pebbles and low-tide sand. It looks out towards Thorn Island and the Milford Haven Waterway.

Roadside parking for about ten cars can be found on the lane to Dale Fort Field Centre at the point where the coastal path leaves the road, but the lane is very narrow and not suitable for wide or long vehicles. Castlebeach is a five-minute walk away, with access from the coastal path which drops down to near beach level. Facing east and flanked by wooded cliffs, it tends to become shady towards late afternoon.

Watwick Bay

GRID REF **SM 817040**
GPS **51.6917°N, 5.1589°W**
COUNTY **Pembrokeshire**
BEACH FACES **East**

Watwick Bay is a sandy beach approximately one mile south of the village of Dale. The shore is firm sand surrounded by low sandstone cliffs,

and looks out towards West Angle Bay on the opposite side of the Milford Haven Waterway. It's sheltered and good for sunbathing, but becomes shady towards late afternoon.

To get there, take the St Ann's Head road from Dale heading south for three quarters of a mile, then follow a public footpath on the left. After a further half a mile heading south, a footpath on the left leads across a short field to the coastal path and continues down to the shore.

Mill Bay

GRID REF **SM 809035**
GPS **51.6869°N, 5.1701°W**
COUNTY **Pembrokeshire**
BEACH FACES **South-east**

Mill Bay is a small beach on the east side of St Ann's Head. A small car park is situated at the end of the road from Dale, and Mill Bay is a short walk back along the coastal path. At low tide the

beach is sandy, with sandstone rocks, streams and rock pools. Access is from the coastal path, which drops down to near beach level.

The remains of the steamship HMS *Barking*, which sank in March 1964 on its way to the scrapyard, can be seen in the sand. On the coastal path to the south of the beach, a plaque commemorates the landing here of Henry Tudor, later Henry VII, and his army on 7 August 1485.

Westdale Bay

GRID REF **SM 799059**
GPS **51.7081°N, 5.1861°W**
COUNTY **Pembrokeshire**
BEACH FACES **West**

The picturesque sandy beach of Westdale Bay lies approximately three quarters of a mile west of Dale. A narrow no through road (the left turning opposite the church) overlooks the bay on the north side, and has very limited space for roadside parking. Alternative parking can be found at a pay & display car park in Dale. Access to Westdale Bay is from Dale Castle, where a footpath leads across a field to the steep coastal path, and then down some wooden steps to the shore.

The beach is bordered by red sandstone pebbles and cliffs, and looks out towards Skokholm Island, about two and a half miles offshore, with Grassholm Island in the far distance. It's a popular surfing beach, at its best on a rising tide but before the high. Strong rips can occur, and rocks can be a hazard, so it's not one for the inexperienced.

2 Marloes Sands

Marloes Sands

GRID REF **SM 784074**
GFS **51.7210°N, 5.2087°W**
COUNTY **Pembrokeshire**
BEACH FACES **South-west**

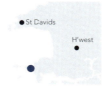

The mile-long crescent of Marloes Sands (pronounced 'Mar-loiss') reaches from Red Cliff at one end to Gateholm Island at the other. It's mostly sand and rock pools, and is a popular location for geologists, anglers and surfers.

Parking is at an attended National Trust car park which is signposted from Marloes village. Toilets can be found a short distance away along a track which begins near the car park entrance, and access to the sands is a ten- to fifteen-minute walk along a gravelled bridleway. There are no facilities at the beach, but Marloes village has a shop, a cafe and a pub. Surf conditions are best on a rising tide with south-west winds. It's generally suitable for novices, and the southern end, away from most of the rocks, is the preferred area.

Albion Sands

GRID REF **SM 771075**
GPS **51.7213°N, 5.2276°W**
COUNTY **Pembrokeshire**
BEACH FACES **South-west**

Albion Sands is a small secluded beach on the north side of Gateholm Island. It gets its name from the paddle steamer *Albion*, which was beached here in April 1837. Parts of the wreck can still be seen at low tide. The beach consists of sand and rocks backed by high, unstable cliffs of mudstone and sandstone. Access is either from Marloes Sands at low tide, or otherwise down a rugged and slightly overgrown path on the promontory.

The nearest parking is the attended National Trust car park for Marloes Sands.

From here the shortest route is to take the footpath towards the youth hostel and continue past Marloes Mere until the track enters a field. Bear left to meet the coastal path after about 140 metres. Turn right and at the next corner a path leads towards the promontory and down to the end of Marloes Sands. Albion Sands is then a short walk over rocks. Be aware of the state of the tide if visiting this beach, as this is the only way off the beach. The next two bays west of Albion Sands – Watery Bay and Victoria Bay – are backed by steep rocks and cliffs, and are not easily accessible.

Marloes Mere is good for birdwatching, often hosting some rare breeding and migrant waders. Gateholm Island was once the site of an Iron Age fort and in those times it was better connected to the mainland. It can be accessed by a scramble up the side facing Albion Sands.

Renny Slip & Martin's Haven

Martin's Haven

GRID REF **SM 760092**
GPS **51.7362°N, 5.2446°W**
COUNTY **Pembrokeshire**
BEACH FACES **North**

Martin's Haven is a small inlet at the north-western end of the Marloes Peninsula, and is the departure point for boat trips to Skomer and Skokholm islands. An attended National Trust car park is about 200 metres away, and access to the shore is a walk down a steep hill. The beach is mostly pebbled, flanked by cliffs of various volcanic rocks. Shore diving, snorkelling and kayaking are popular activities, but very little beach is available at high tide. Facilities include toilets, the Lockley Lodge Visitor Centre and an emergency telephone, and dogs are allowed at all times. The car park is listed as a Dark Sky discovery site – a place away from light pollution suitable for stargazing at night.

Renny Slip is on the opposite side of the peninsula and is a beach of rocks, rock pools, shingle and some low-tide sand backed by high unstable cliffs. It looks out towards Skokholm Island, which is two and a half miles offshore. Access from the coast path is a scramble down a very steep zigzag path on the south side of the neck of the headland. Care needs to be taken if descending to this beach. Dogs are allowed, but may need some help at the top of the path.

Musselwick Sands

GRID REF **SM 785090**
GPS **51.7354°N, 5.2083°W**
COUNTY **Pembrokeshire**
BEACH FACES **North-west**

Musselwick Sands is on the north side of the Marloes Peninsula. Roadside parking for a few cars is available on the north side at Martin's Haven Road, just west of Marloes village. Beach access is a walk of about 350 metres along a public footpath. The last section is fairly steep, with steps cut into the rock on the final descent. At high tide this is as far as you can get but low tide reveals a long sandy beach stretching in both directions, backed by high cliffs of black mudstone to the west and red sandstone to the east. There is only one way on and off this beach, and both sides can be cut off by the incoming tide.

St Brides Haven

GRID REF **SM 801111**
GPS **51.7548°N, 5.1865°W**
COUNTY **Pembrokeshire**
BEACH FACES **North**

St Brides Haven is a small bay of sand and pebbles just below St Brides Church, at the southern end of St Brides Bay. The shingle and low cliffs are of red sandstone and mudstone. Facilities include toilets and picnic tables, and parking is on grass in front of the church. Access to the shore is then down a short track. This is a popular beach with scuba divers, being very sheltered and suitable for novices.

Mill Haven

GRID REF **SM 816123**
GPS **51.7662°N, 5.1655°W**
COUNTY **Pembrokeshire**
BEACH FACES **North-west**

Mill Haven is situated on the coastal path north of the Marloes Peninsula. Access is along the coastal path for either one or two miles, from St Brides Haven or Little Haven respectively. The beach looks out towards Stack Rocks about half a mile offshore, and consists of pebbles and red sandstone rocks.

Little Haven & The Settlands

Little Haven

GRID REF **SM 856130**
GPS **51.7740°N, 5.1081°W**
COUNTY **Pembrokeshire**
BEACH FACES **North-west**

Little Haven nestles in a steep-sided valley bordering St Brides Bay. The beach is sandy with rock pools, and is flanked by cliffs of shale and sandstone. A slipway gives access to the shore, and facilities nearby include a shop, pubs, toilets and a pay & display car park. Swimming and surfing are generally safe, and the beach is well suited to novice surfers.

A wide, wheelchair-accessible path on the south side of Little Haven leads to a viewpoint known as The Lookout, south of which are the two small adjoining coves of the Sheep Wash and Rook's Bay. These are mostly rocky, with small amounts of low tide sand. At low tide it's possible to walk around the northern headland to Broad Haven and the Settlands beach, which is a wide, sandy beach backed by shingle and high cliffs. It is not accessible from the coastal path.

Broad Haven

GRID REF **SM 858137**
GPS **51.7804°N, 5.1056°W**
COUNTY **Pembrokeshire**
BEACH FACES **West**

The wide beach of Broad Haven lies within the larger St Brides Bay. The shore is firm, golden sand backed by a sea wall and flanked by cliffs of sandstone and shale. More sheltered for surfing than Newgale Sands (see page 118), it is best on a rising tide and has cleaner, smaller surf.

Parking is at one of two pay & display car parks: a small one on the seafront (Marine Road) and a larger one on Millmoor Way (just off the B4341 Haverfordwest Road). Access to the shore is down steps, a ramp or a slipway. Facilities include toilets, a pub, cafes, takeaways, a post office and a surf shop. Lifeguards are on duty during July and August, and dog restrictions apply on the northern section of the beach from 1 May to 30 September.

Druidston Haven & Madoc's Haven

Druidston Haven is a sandy beach between Newgale Sands and Broad Haven. It sits on the eastern side of St Brides Bay and can be reached along a singletrack lane. Some roadside parking is available where the width of the lane permits, but spaces are very limited and traffic problems are likely during busy periods. Access to the shore is down a wide stony path which emerges on the pebble bank at the beach's rear. At high tide the sand is completely covered, but at low tide the beach is wide and sandy, with shale headlands containing graptolite fossils.

Madoc's Haven is a beach of sand, rock pools and caves. Lying at the northern end of Druidston Haven, it can only be easily reached along the shore for about an hour and a half either side of low tide. Surf conditions are similar to Newgale, but the waves tend to be slightly smaller and best between low and mid tide. There can also be strong currents around low tide.

Nolton Haven

GRID REF **SM 858184**
GPS **51.8226°N, 5.1085°W**
CCUNTY **Pembrokeshire**
BEACH FACES **West**

Nolton Haven is a small sheltered bay south of Newgale Sands. A free car park is located just behind the beach, and from there a short concrete slipway gives access to the shore. The beach is mostly sand, flanked by high cliffs of sandstone, siltstone and coal veins. From mid to high tide it's a good beach for sunbathing and swimming, but rips can occur on a low tide, especially on the northern side of the bay. Facilities include toilets and a pub. Lifeguards patrol from late June until early September.

Newgale Sands

GRID REF **SM 848216**
GPS **51.8509°N, 5.1250°W**
COUNTY **Pembrokeshire**
BEACH FACES **West**

St Davids
H'west

Newgale is a popular surfing beach on Pembrokeshire's west coast. Approximately two miles long, it's mostly fine sand backed by a storm bank of pebbles. At the northern end, the stream of Brandy Brook percolates through the pebble bank on to the beach, while towards the south the small headland of Maidenhall Point has a walk-through cave. Further south are some smaller coves with rock pools.

Parking is at one of two pay & display car parks positioned just behind the beach. Alternative parking is available in lay-bys on the descent into Newgale from Haverfordwest and also on Welsh Road at the far southern end. The section of beach joined by the two car parks is subject to dog restrictions from 1 May to 30 September, and lifeguards patrol in front of both car parks from June to September. Facilities include a surf shop, a pub, a cafe, a campsite and toilets. Surf conditions are usually reliable, making it a good beach for beginners, but it's best to avoid high water when the waves hit the pebble bank.

Pen-y-Cwm Beach & Cwm bach

Pen-y-Cwm Beach

GRID REF **SM 843227**
GPS **51.8606°N, 5.1330°W**
COUNTY **Pembrokeshire**
BEACH FACES **West**

Pen-y-Cwm Beach lies at the northern end of Newgale Sands, the north-east corner of St Brides Bay. At low tide it can be reached along the shore from Newgale, and at other times via the coastal path. Alternatively it can be reached by a public footpath from Pen-y-Cwm, where roadside parking can be found.

The shore is coarse sand and light shingle, with rocks, rock pools and a walk through cave. The surrounding cliffs are of conglomerate, shale and purple sandstone. Look out for Skomer Island to the left and Grassholm Island straight ahead – some seventeen miles offshore.

Just to the north is the small, sandy cove of Cwm bach. Backed by high cliffs, it can only be reached along the shore on a low tide.

Porthmynawyd

GRID REF **SM 826228**
GPS **51.8609°N, 5.1577°W**
COUNTY **Pembrokeshire**
BEACH FACES **South**
🅿

Porthmynawyd (pronounced 'Porth-min-arwid') is a small, sandy cove flanked by high cliffs. The headland of Dinas Fach on the west side shelters the bay, while the eastern side has a

long cave which can be explored on a low tide. Most of the sand is covered between mid and high tide.

Lay-by parking is available on the A487 either side of the Pointz Castle turning, at grid ref: SM 832238 (GPS: 51.8705°N, 5.1494°W). Access is by public footpath through Pointz Castle Farm. At the sharp bend the beach path continues ahead through two fields, thence along a steep-sided valley to the beach. Keep to the right across the first field and to the left across the second.

Gwadn

GRID REF **SM 802236**
GPS **51.8671°N, 5.1930°W**
COUNTY **Pembrokeshire**
BEACH FACES **South-west**

Gwadn is a small, sandy cove in a steep-sided valley just east of Solva Harbour. Very sheltered, it's good for sunbathing and high-tide swimming. Much of the valley behind has slowly silted up, unlike neighbouring Solva, and is now marshland. Access is either along the shore from Solva at low tide or via the coastal path at the back of the beach.

3 Solva Harbour, view from above   **4** Solva Harbour, looking up the beach   **5** Solva Harbour

Solva Harbour

GRID REF **SM 804241**
GPS **51.8710°N, 5.1946°W**
COUNTY **Pembrokeshire**
BEACH FACES **South-west**

● St Davids

● H'west

Solva Harbour is an example of a ria – a glacial meltwater channel now open to the sea. At low tide it's a long sandy inlet, flanked by cliffs with a few old lime kilns on the eastern side. Very little sand is available at high tide, but it's generally safe for swimming.

There is a small attended car park, from which access to the shore is down a slipway, but it fills up quickly in summer. Some additional parking can be found up the hill to the west. Facilities include toilets, cycle stands, a pub and a cafe. Further pubs, restaurants and craft shops can be found in the village.

The headland on the eastern side is known as The Gribbin and has excellent views. On the other side of this is Gwadn Cove, which can be reached either along the shore at low tide or via the coastal path. Just offshore are the islands of Green Scar and Black Scar.

Aber Llong & Porth y Rhaw

GRID REF **SM 787241**
GPS **51.8710°N, 5.2150°W**
COUNTY **Pembrokeshire**
BEACH FACES **South-west**

● St Davids
H'west

One of Pembrokeshire's least visited beaches, Aber Llong is mostly rocky with a cove of sand and shingle to the west side. The high cliffs which back it provide good shelter from winds and the rusting remains of a shipwreck are visible at low tide. Access is possible by walking (with great care) down a steep scree slope and rocks at the back of the beach.

Porth y Rhaw ('Rhaw' rhymes with 'cow') is a small inlet just west of Aber Llong. The cliffs are comprised of dark mudstone and sandstone, with rocks, pebbles and some low-tide sand making up the shore. It's probably a good place for snorkelling and fishing, but not much else.

Parking for about six or seven cars can be found on the lane to Nine Wells Caravan and Camping Site: turn off the St Davids road just after the 'Nine Wells' sign where the road dips. The parking area is about forty metres down on the left, just after the cottage at grid ref: SM 787248 (GPS: 51.8768°N, 5.2122°W). From here a footpath follows the valley to Porth y Rhaw, and Aber Llong is a short distance eastwards along the coastal path.

1

Caer Bwdy Bay

GRID REF **SM 766243**
GPS **51.8720°N, 5.2456°W**
COUNTY **Pembrokeshire**
BEACH FACES **South**
Ⓟ

Just a short walk east from Caerfai Bay is
the small National Trust cove of Caer Bwdy

(pronounced 'Kiy-er boo-dee'). The shore is
of rocks, pebbles and some low-tide sand,
flanked by purple sandstone cliffs. The closest
parking is about a hundred metres along a lane
(signposted 'Trelerw' from the A487), where a
small parking area can be found next to the
National Trust's Caer Bwdy pillar at grid ref:
SM 769248 (GPS: 51.8766°N, 5.2416°W). A little
further along the lane, a public footpath forks
off to the right and leads to the beach.

Caerfai Bay

GRID REF **SM 760242**
GPS **51.8708°N, 5.2543°W**
COUNTY **Pembrokeshire**
BEACH FACES **South**
🌊

Reached along a narrow lane from the A487
just south of St Davids, Caerfai Bay is a popular
sandy beach backed by cliffs of green and
purple sandstone. A free clifftop car park

overlooks the bay. Access to the shore from
here is down a fairly steep, concrete path with
some steps.

Sheltered and south facing, this is a good
place for sunbathing, with caves and rock pools
to explore. Swimming is generally safe within
the bay, but there can be strong currents at low
tide. At high tide most of the sand is covered.

There are no facilities at the beach, but
the National Park Information Centre at the
St Davids end of the lane has pay & display
parking, toilets and a cafe.

Porth y Ffynnon & Porthclais

Porthclais

GRID REF **SM 742239**
GPS **51.8674°N, 5.2802°W**
COUNTY **Pembrokeshire**
BEACH FACES **South**

The tiny River Alun enters the sea at Porthclais, which was once an important port for St Davids and the surrounding area. The steep-sided inlet is protected by a harbour wall at its entrance and has a small low-tide beach just outside. It's a popular venue for kayaking, scuba diving and sailing. East of the harbour, a rock slab

provides training for novice climbers. Facilities include two small car parks, toilets and a small refreshment kiosk.

The next cove to the east is Porth y Ffynnon, a beach of purple sandstone rocks and some sand backed by high cliffs. It's only accessible from land on exceptionally low tides, but even then this will involve some clambering over slippery rocks and wading through rock pools. To reach it, head down to sea level just east of the National Trust 'Porthclais' sign, taking care to keep a safe distance from any sheer drops. When at sea level and if the tide is low enough, you should be able to work your way around to the beach. Once there a close eye will need to be kept on the tide.

4 Porthlysgi Bay, shore level   5 Porthlysgi Bay   6 Porthlysgi (left) & Porth Coch Bach (right)

Porth Coch Bach & Porthlysgi

Porthlysgi

GRID REF **SM 730236**
GPS **51.8642°N, 5.2974°W**
COUNTY **Pembrokeshire**
BEACH FACES **South-west**

St Davids

H'west

Porthlysgi Bay (pronounced 'Porth-lissgy') is a quiet beach one and a half miles south-west of St Davids. The shore is sandy at low tide, backed by shingle, and looks out to the small craggy islet of Carreg yr Esgob (Bishop Rock)

just offshore. On the east side, the secluded cove of Porth Coch Bach can be reached by walking over the rocks, or wading at low tide. Being very sheltered, it's good for sunbathing and swimming. Access is from the coastal path which runs for a few metres along the back of the beach.

The nearest parking is an attended car park at Porthclais at grid ref: SM 739242 (GPS: 51.8707°N, 5.2854°W). From here Porthlysgi can be reached via the coastal path, but there is a shorter route along the track opposite the car park that meets the coastal path near Porthlysgi Farm.

Porthselau

GRID REF **SM 726260**
GPS **51.8856°N, 5.3048°W**
COUNTY **Pembrokeshire**
BEACH FACES **North-west**

Lying just three quarters of a mile south of Whitesands Bay, Porthselau is a small, sandy cove flanked by cliffs of sandstone and conglomerate. Access from the coastal path is down a few steps cut into the rock or along the shore from Whitesands Bay at low tide. A pay & display car park is located on the St Davids to St Justinian's road at grid ref: SM 729253 (GPS: 51.8798°N, 5.3000°W), and further lay-by parking can be found towards the end of this road, but spaces here are quickly taken. Alternative parking is at Whitesands. A public footpath runs through Pencarnan Farm Caravan and Camping site to the beach. It's generally a safe beach for swimming.

2 Whitesands Bay, beach and car park **3** Porth Lleuog and Carn Llidi **4** Whitesands Bay

Whitesands Bay & Porth Lleuog

Whitesands Bay

GR'D REF **SM 731271**
GPS **51.8957°N, 5.2982°W**
COUNTY **Pembrokeshire**
BEACH FACES **West**

●● St Davids

H'west
●

Located about two miles west of St Davids, Whitesands Bay is regarded as one of the best surf beaches in Wales, occasionally producing waves up to three metres. The sandy shore is backed by low dunes and boulder clay cliffs. Bounded on the north side by the headland of Trwynhwrddyn, the small sandy cove of Porth Lleuog is just on the other side. The beaches look out towards Ramsey Island and the Bishops and Clerks reefs and are overlooked by the 181-metre rocky peak of Carn Llidi.

An attended car park is behind the beach, access to which is down a slipway, and facilities include toilets, drinking water, picnic tables, cycle stands and a cafe. Surf conditions are best between mid and high tide and the area in front of the car park is the most popular, but a rip current can occur near the Trwynhwrddyn headland. Lifeguards patrol daily from late May until early September, and also weekends from Easter until October. A total dog ban operates from 1 May to 30 September. Dogs are allowed on Porth Lleuog.

1 **Porthmelgan,** looking towards Carn Llidi   2 **Porthmelgan,** from the coastal path
3 **Aberpwll**   4 **Abereiddy Bay,** beach and car park

Porthmelgan

GRID REF **SM 727278**
GPS **51.9018°N, 5.3045°W**
CCUNTY **Pembrokeshire**
BEACH FACES **South-west**

Situated between St Davids Head and Whitesands, Porthmelgan is a secluded, sandy beach flanked by high cliffs. It looks out towards Ramsey Island and the Bishops and Clerks reefs. Strong currents mean it's not a good beach for swimming, particularly in surf conditions. The closest parking is at Whitesands.

Aberpwll

GRID REF **SM 784306**
GPS **51.9292°N, 5.2236°W**
COUNTY **Pembrokeshire**
BEACH FACES **North**

Aberpwll is a small pebbly cove, flanked by shale cliffs. Two small streams emerge on to the beach and flow over the pebbles. A good place to go for snorkelling or wild swimming, there are caves and lagoons to be explored just outside the cove.

Abereiddy Bay

GRID REF **SM 794313**
GPS **51.9359°N, 5.2095°W**
COUNTY **Pembrokeshire**
BEACH FACES **West**

Located on Pembrokeshire's north-west coast, Abereiddy Bay (pronounced 'Abber-aythee') has a shore of shingle and dark sand flanked by shale cliffs. The car park overlooks the beach and fills up quickly in summer. Refreshments are usually available from catering vans. On the north side are the ruins of quarrymen's cottages known as Tne Street, and a toilet block is set a little further back.

Just north of the beach, a wide path leads to a flooded slate quarry known as the Blue Lagoon, which has jumps of up to seven metres into the water. Signs warn that the water is cold and twenty-five metres deep.

Traeth Llyfn

GRID REF **SM 802320**
GPS **51.9425°N, 5.1983°W**
COUNTY **Pembrokeshire**
BEACH FACES **West**

On Pembrokeshire's rocky north-west coast, Traeth Llyfn is a secluded bay of sand and some pebbles, backed by shale cliffs. Access from the coastal path is down a long flight of 133 metal and concrete steps.

The bay is generally safe for swimming, but a rip current can occur on the south side. The steps are the only way on and off the beach, so an eye needs to be kept on the incoming tide. Dogs are allowed at all times but may have to be carried down the open-tread steps on the metal stairway.

Porthgain

GRID REF **SM 814325**
GPS **51.9475°N, 5.1812°W**
COUNTY **Pembrokeshire**
BEACH FACES **North-west**

Built to serve the brickworks and quarries to the west, Porthgain is more of a harbour than a beach. There's some low-tide sand within the harbour walls, while immediately outside is a sheltered inlet. Facilities at the small village include free parking (some overlooking the harbour), a pub, a cafe, a slipway and toilets.

Aberfelin

GRID REF **SM 832325**
GPS **51.9482°N, 5.1551°W**
COUNTY **Pembrokeshire**
BEACH FACES **North-west**

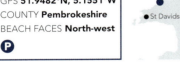

Aberfelin, also known as Aberdraw, is a rocky cove near the village of Trefin. Backed by the ruins of an old water mill, the beach consists of rocks and rock pools, though swimming is not recommended due to strong currents. The road which passes just behind the beach has limited roadside parking, and though there are no facilities here Trefin is a short walk away and has toilets, a pub and a shop.

Abercastle

GRID REF **SM 852337**
GPS **51.9597°N, 5.1268°W**
COUNTY **Pembrokeshire**
BEACH FACES **West**

St Davids
H'west

Abercastle is a small harbour and beach on Pembrokeshire's north coast. A very small parking area with toilets overlooks the shore,

and access is down a short slipway. The lower shore is mostly seaweed-strewn sand, with the headland on the west side becoming an island on the high tide.

This sheltered beach, a short walk away from Trefin village, is popular with anglers, canoeists and divers. West of the bay are the fragmented remains of the *SS Leysian*, a steamship which hit rocks in February 1917 on its way to Barry, which are located west of the bay at a depth of about fifteen metres.

Pwllstrodur

GRID REF **SM 865338**
GPS **51.9611°N, 5.1079°W**
COUNTY **Pembrokeshire**
BEACH FACES **North**

St Davids

Pwllstrodur is a small, secluded cove between Abermawr and Abercastle. The shore consists of dark sand and slate pebbles, flanked by cliffs of shale. Access is via the coastal path, or for an easier route take the road out of Abercastle and follow the farm road on the left on foot for about half a mile. After this take a public footpath on the left through a field to the beach.

Abermawr & Aberbach

Abermawr

GRID REF **SM 882347**
GPS **51.9699°N, 5.0838°W**
COUNTY **Pembrokeshire**
BEACH FACES **West**

....

Aberbach

GRID REF **SM 883350**
GPS **51.9726°N, 5.0825°W**
COUNTY **Pembrokeshire**
BEACH FACES **West**

● St Davids

● H'west

Abermawr and Aberbach are two neighbouring beaches separated by a small headland on Pembrokeshire's north-west coast, just off the A487. The beaches are flanked by low cliffs of boulder clay and mudstone, and backed by pebble banks which have blocked off the valleys behind, creating marshland. The coastal path runs along the top of the pebble banks.

Whereas Aberbach is mostly pebbles with a small stream, but very little sand, Abermawr is mostly sand and is a popular surfing beach. As it needs a good swell to work, it is best to visit Abermawr between low and mid tide, and when other beaches are blown out. Be wary of strong currents.

Roadside parking is available on a no through road signposted 'Abermawr', which has a turning circle at its end.

Porth Dwgan

GRID REF **SM 882352**
GPS **51.9744°N, 5.0841°W**
COUNTY **Pembrokeshire**
BEACH FACES **West**

Lying just north of Aberbach, Porth Dwgan (originally Porth Duggan) is one of Pembrokeshire's secret beaches. There is even a secret access; though from most angles it appears to be inaccessible, low-tide access is possible via a short cave between this beach and the narrow rocky inlet to the north. The cave emerges on the rocks at the side of Porth Dwgan, and more clambering over rocks is necessary to reach the shore. Once on the shore you may notice local coasteering clubs, which the pebbly beach is popular with. However, take care not to get cut off by the tide visiting this beach.

Just outside the cove on the south side lies the wreck of the 800-ton sailing ship, the *Charles Holmes*, one of many ships which sank in the Great Storm of 25 October 1859.

Pwllcrochan Bay

GRID REF **SM 884364**
GPS **51.9852°N, 5.0819°W**
COUNTY **Pembrokeshire**
BEACH FACES **West**

Access is down a steep path on the southern side, which provides the view seen in the photo. As part of the original path has been lost to erosion the final seven metres is a climb down the rocks. This climb is not difficult and there is usually a rope to hold on to.

Note that the larger part of the beach is only accessible around low tide. The nearest roadside parking is at Abermawr, approximately a mile to the south.

Pwllcrochan is a remote bay with a dark sandy shore, backed by high cliffs and sheltered on the north by the headland of Trwyn Llwyd.

1 Porth Maenmelyn, at mid tide   **2** Porth Maenmelyn, the path up from the beach   **3** Porth Maenmelyn

Porth Maenmelyn

GRID REF **SM 887392**
GPS **52.0105°N, 5.0793°W**
COUNTY **Pembrokeshire**
BEACH FACES **West**

Fishguard

● St Davids

Porth Maenmelyn lies south of Strumble Head, and its rocky, dark sand is backed by high cliffs of soft mudstone. A steep, narrow path down, which is not a right of way, was cut into the cliffs many years ago and has since become very

dangerous to use. **Do not attempt to visit this beach unless you are absolutely certain you can do so safely.**

A small parking area with space for approximately ten cars is at Pwll Deri at grid ref: SM 893386 (GPS: 52.0059°N, 5.0706°W). From here take the coastal path northwards to its lowest point behind the beach. A short path then leads to a narrow cutting through the side of the cliffs, beyond which the path is covered with piles of loose slate with sheer drops to the side. A rope will be required from this point.

4 Porth Sychan, looking north   **5** Porth Sychan, from the coastal path

Porth Sychan

GRID REF **SM 905408**
GPS **52.0255°N, 5.0541°W**
COUNTY **Pembrokeshire**
BEACH FACES **North**

Fishguard

● St Davids

Between Stumble Head and Fishguard, the only accessible part of the shore is Porth Sychan.

A secluded bay of pebbles, shingle and seaweed-covered rocks, it has three small streams emerging on to the shore. Parking is at Strumble Head, about a mile to the west at grid ref: SM 895412 (GPS: 52.0296°N, 5.0699°W), where the free parking area overlooks the sea. Access is then from the coastal path which drops down to near beach level.

Fishguard Beaches

Goodwick Sands

GRID REF **SM 949378**
GPS **52.0002°N, 4.9882°W**
COUNTY **Pembrokeshire**
BEACH FACES **North-east**

West of Fishguard town, Goodwick Sands is a beach of shingle, mussel shells and some coarse sand, with a lower shore of seaweed-strewn rocks. A sea wall of boulders backs the beach as well as the main A40 to Fishguard Harbour. Toilets and a pub are nearby, while a few hundred metres away, a modern building houses a cafe. A few parking spaces overlook the beach, but a larger car park is on the opposite side of the A40.

The town of Fishguard is a short distance to the east, and has a leisure centre with a twenty-five-metre pool if you don't fancy braving the seawater. Fishguard & Goodwick Railway Station is within easy walking distance, although it has a very limited service, and dog restrictions apply on the section of the beach nearest the breakwater from 1 May to 30 September.

Pwll Hir, found at grid ref: SM 950397 (GPS: 52.0176°N, 4.9881°W), is a small cove of pebbles just north of the ferry terminal. It falls within the boundaries of Fishguard Port, and there is no public access.

The small, sandy cove of Lampit, found at grid ref: SM 959374 (GPS: 51.9980°N, GPS: 4.9743°W), lies on the west side of the old harbour, and can be reached by a good path and steep steps or along the shore from the A487 bridge.

Pwll Landdu & Pwll Edyrn

Pwll Landdu

GRID REF **SM 966377**
GPS **51.9999°N, 4.9634°W**
COUNTY **Pembrokeshire**
BEACH FACES **North**

Pwll Landdu, or Black Shore Pool, is the only accessible part of the shore between Fishguard and Aberbach. Access is a short, steep path from the coastal path, down to the pebbly beach.

On the eastern side is a small cave, and at low tide a gap in the rocks leads to Pwll Edyrn, a similar but more secluded cove approximately forty metres wide, backed by steep banks. The nearest parking is a lay-by on the A487 east of Fishguard, grid ref: SM 962376 (GPS: 51.9990°N, 4.9697°W).

139

Aber Bach

GRID REF **SM 997387**
GPS **52.0101°N, 4.9189°W**
COUNTY **Pembrokeshire**
BEACH FACES **North**

Aber Bach is a small cove of pebbles and low-tide sand, three miles east of Fishguard. Access

is a walk of half a mile along public footpaths from Dinas Cross. Parking is on the north side of the A487 opposite the tennis court, at grid ref: SN 003382 (GPS: 52.0070°N, 4.9098°W). From here, facing north, take the bridleway to the left until it reaches a narrow lane, bearing in mind that this bridleway shares its route with a small stream for about ten metres. Turn left down the hill, then right along a track just before crossing the stream at the bottom.

Pwll Gwylog

GRID REF **SM 999394**
GPS **52.0164°N, 4.9164°W**
COUNTY **Pembrokeshire**
BEACH FACES **North-west**

One of Pembrokeshire's secret beaches, Pwll Gwylog, which translates as 'Guillemot Pool', is just a short walk away from the much busier Pwllgwaelod. The shore is of shingle and some gravelly sand, flanked by crumbling slate cliffs. The shingle bank at the back of the beach is made up mostly of rounded pieces of slate, ideal for skimming.

Access from the coastal path is down a steep path to the eastern side, and the nearest parking is at Pwllgwaelod.

Pwllgwaelod

GRID REF **SN 003399**
GPS **52.0210°N, 4.9109°W**
COUNTY **Pembrokeshire**
BEACH FACES **West**

although it fills up quickly, and access to the shore is down a slipway. Generally safe for swimming and sheltered for sunbathing, this beach also has toilets, drinking water and a pub.

An asphalt footpath suitable for anything with wheels leads through the sheltered Cwm Dewi valley to Cwm-yr-Eglwys on the other side of Dinas Island. The Pembrokeshire Coast Path skirts Dinas Island, providing an alternative and more strenuous return route.

Lying on the west side of Dinas Island, Pwllgwaelod is a small cove of dark sand. A small, free car park is just behind the beach,

Cwm-yr-Eglwys & Aber Gwyn

Cwm-yr-Eglwys

GRID REF **SN 016401**
GPS **52.0233°N, 4.8921°W**
COUNTY **Pembrokeshire**
BEACH FACES **North-east**

Cwm-yr-Eglwys, pronounced 'Koomer-egg-lewis', is a small beach on Pembrokeshire's north

coast. Immediately behind lie the remains of St Brynach's church, which was destroyed in the Great Storm of 1859. Further back is a caravan site and pay & display car park with toilets.

The shore is of sand and pebbles, and access is down a slipway. Little beach is available at high tide, but swimming is generally safe within the bay.

On the eastern side the cove of Aber Gwyn can be reached by walking over the rocks at low tide, or by a 200-metre swim.

Aberfforest

GRID REF **SN 026396**
GPS **52.0192°N, 4.8772°W**
COUNTY **Pembrokeshire**
BEACH FACES **North**

Situated between Dinas Head and Newport, Aberfforest is a small cove of low-tide sand

backed by shingle. Some holiday homes overlook it, but it is sheltered and generally safe for swimming at high tide. Lay-by parking is available on both sides of the A487 at grid ref: SN 028387 (GPS: 52.0124°N, 4.8740°W), and from here a public footpath signposted 'Aberfforest' reaches almost to the beach. Alternative access is along the coastal path from Cwm-yr-Eglwys.

About 200 metres behind the beach is a waterfall set in a wooded valley, which is certainly worth the short walk.

Aber Rhigian

GRID REF **SN 032396**
GPS **52.0194°N, 4.8685°W**
COUNTY **Pembrokeshire**
BEACH FACES **North**

Aber Rhigian is a remote bay of dark sand with low cliffs, backed by a pebble bank which carries the coastal path. Parking is available on the

A487 at grid ref: SN 039389 (GPS: 52.0144°N, 4.8588°W). From here, follow the narrow track leading towards the coast. After 200 metres turn left along a similar track. Immediately before the gates to a house, the path turns right into an area of ancient woodland, closely following a lively stream.

Alternative access to Aber Rhigian is via the coastal path from Newport. Swimming within the bay is generally safe.

Parrog Beach & Newport Sands

Newport Sands

GRID REF **SN 054405**
GPS **52.0282°N, 4.8370°W**
COUNTY **Pembrokeshire**
BEACH FACES **West**

Newport Sands is a mile-long sandy beach on the north side of the River Nevern. An attended car park overlooks the beach, and parking is also allowed on the sand. Lay-by parking is available

outside of Newport village on either end of the Nevern bridge. From here the coastal path follows the river about three quarters of a mile to the beach, which looks out towards Dinas Head. Access is down a slipway.

The northern end of the beach is rockier, with cliffs and a small waterfall. To the south the sand continues alongside the river, which on a low tide can be waded across to Newport's Parrog Beach – a small beach of sand, shingle and some mud. Beach facilities include toilets, drinking water, cycle stands and a cafe. Lifeguards are on duty from late June until early September.

Ceibwr Bay

GRID REF **SN 109458**
GPS **52.0778°N, 4.7598°W**
COUNTY **Pembrokeshire**
BEACH FACES **North-west**

Ceibwr Bay is a National Trust beach, reached by a narrow lane along the Nant Ceibwr valley from the village of Moylegrove.

The pebbly shore is crossed by a small stream and flanked by cliffs of sandstone and mudstone. Approximately two thirds of a mile south-west along the coastal path is the Witches' Cauldron, or Pwll-y-Wrach, a collapsed cave formed by erosion of soft shale rocks.

Parking is at the roadside, with space for twenty to twenty-five vehicles. There are no facilities, but nearby Moylegrove has a small car park with toilets.

Poppit Sands

GRID REF **SN 152486**
GPS **52.1044°N, 4.6987°W**
COUNTY **Pembrokeshire**
BEACH FACES **North-east**

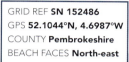

Cardigan

Newport

Poppit Sands stands two miles north-west of Cardigan on the Teifi Estuary. A pay & display car park is just behind the beach and access is a short, level boardwalk. The sandy shore is backed mainly by low dunes, becoming rocky towards the north-western end. The beach looks out towards Cardigan Island and the village of Gwbert on the opposite side of the Teifi.

Facilities include toilets, a cafe and a small picnic area. Lifeguards patrol from mid June until early September, and dog restrictions apply on the western half of the beach from 1 May to 30 September. For surfers, Poppit is a beach break, surfable at most stages of the tide and generally suitable for beginners. A sandbar break on the Gwbert side of the estuary is for the more experienced and can be surfed on a rising tide, but strong rips occur here.

The county of Ceredigion (pronounced 'Kerrer-diggy-on') is bounded by the rivers Teifi to the south and the Dyfi to the north. The terrain is very hilly, and the coastal path particularly so, with three stretches going for several miles without encountering any towns or villages.

The county's southern shore faces north-west and is mostly rocky, with small, sandy bays. Proceeding north, the west-facing beaches become longer, and are usually good for surfing; lifeguards patrol the main beaches in summer. Aberystwyth is the main resort and university town, and the terminus of the Cambrian Coast Line railway and the narrow gauge of the Vale of Rheidol line.

CEREDIGION

Opposite Llanrhystud, watching the sunset

Patch Beach

GRID REF **SN 164485**
GPS **52.1039°N, 4.6811°W**
COUNTY **Ceredigion**
BEACH FACES **South-west**

For a short distance the B4548 Cardigan to Gwbert road runs alongside the Teifi estuary; the adjacent sandy shore is known as Patch Beach. Parking is either at the roadside or by following a short track on to the back of the beach, but swimming is not advisable here due to currents. Better, sandy areas can be found further towards Gwbert.

Evelyn's Beach & Cowley Beach

Evelyn's Beach

GRID REF **SN 160499**
GPS **52.1174°N, 4.6877°W**
COUNTY **Ceredigion**
BEACH FACES **West**

The clifftop hamlet of Gwbert (pronounced 'Goo-bert') lies two and a half miles north of the county town of Cardigan. It has a few unimpressive coves which can be reached along footpaths from the Cliff Hotel. From the car park on the south side of the Cliff Hotel, a signposted and slightly overgrown path leads down to Evelyn's Beach – a tiny cove of some sand, flanked by shale cliffs. On the other side of the hotel, just before an old lime kiln, a short path leads down to the equally disappointing Cowley Beach.

Morgan's Beach

GRID REF **SN 160503**
GPS **52.1210°N, 4.6890°W**
COUNTY **Ceredigion**
BEACH FACES **West**

The best of Gwbert's beaches is Morgan's Beach, a small cove of coarse sand backed by slate cliffs. The furthest beach from Gwbert, it is reached by taking the path northwards from the Cliff Hotel. Access is on the west side, down a short path with steps cut into the rock.

1 Mwnt Beach, looking towards Cardigan Island   **2** Mwnt Beach, access to the beach   **3** Mwnt Beach

Mwnt Beach

GRID REF **SN 194519**
GPS **52.1354°N, 4.6411°W**
COUNTY **Ceredigion**
BEACH FACES **West**

Cardigan

Newport

Mwnt is a small, sandy beach owned by the National Trust. Sheltered by high cliffs, it is good for sunbathing and generally safe for swimming. A narrow no through road leads to the clifftop pay & display car park, which has good views along the coast.

Facilities include toilets and a beach shop, and access to the shore is down a concrete path with approximately 140 steps. Dogs are not allowed on Mwnt Beach from May to September inclusive.

North of the beach is the seventy-five-metre hill of Foel y Mwnt, which has views as far as Snowdonia, and nearby is the small, whitewashed Church of the Holy Cross.

Traeth Gwrddon

GRID REF **SN 233520**
GPS **52.1375°N, 4.5823°W**
COUNTY **Ceredigion**
BEACH FACES **North-west**
❗

Cardigan

Newport

It often seems that the best beaches are the most difficult to get to, and this secret cove near Aberporth is no exception. The nearest roadside parking is at Parcllyn, at grid ref: SN 244513 (GPS: 52.1325°N, 4.5662°W). From here,

it's a good three-quarters-of-a-mile walk along the coastal path, which after an inland diversion around the Defence Evaluation and Research Agency (DERA) site, runs high along the top of a valley which bypasses this tiny cove.

A steep path, which is easily missed, descends the narrow valley. At one time there was a small settlement here, and steps have been cut into the rocks to make the final descent easier, but some climbing is necessary for the last few metres. Low tide reveals a sandy beach flanked by shale cliffs, with a small stream purling down the rocks on to the shore.

Cribach Bay

GRID REF **SN 251522**
GPS **52.1399°N, 4.5561°W**
COUNTY **Ceredigion**
BEACH FACES **North-east**

Lying south of Pencribach Head, Cribach Bay falls within the boundaries of the DERA site at Aberporth; **there is no public access**, either from the land or along the shore. The beach is mostly sandy, surrounded by high slate cliffs.

Aberporth

GRID REF **SN 259515**
GPS **52.1339°N, 4.5441°W**
COUNTY **Ceredigion**
BEACH FACES **North**

Situated between the headlands of Trecregyn and Fathgarreg, Aberporth has a large, sandy beach which separates into two bays at high tide. Dolwen is the western bay, and is the better beach for swimming and sunbathing. Dyffryn is the larger, with a stream (Nant Howni) flowing along its eastern side.

Further east, a few rocky coves can be reached from the coastal path. A small car park is situated just above the beach and further parking is available in the village. Slipways provide access to both beaches. Facilities include toilets, cafes and pubs. Lifeguards patrol in summer and a dog ban operates on Dolwen Beach from 1 May to 30 September. Surf conditions are best around low to mid tide, with south-west winds and a big swell. As it is sheltered, it is generally suitable for beginners, and is worth a try when other beaches are blown out.

Tresaith

GRID REF **SN 279517**
GPS **52.1363°N, 4.5150°W**
COUNTY **Ceredigion**
BEACH FACES **North**

Cardigan

Newport

Just over a mile east of Aberporth, Tresaith has a sandy beach flanked by high shale cliffs. On the west side are the rocks of Carreg-y-Ddafad, and to the east the Afon Saith tumbles on to the shore in a waterfall. Penbryn Beach is about a mile further east, and can be reached along the shore at low tide.

Facilities include toilets, a cafe and a seafront pub. Parking is in a field at the top of the hill, and access to the beach is then down a steep hill and slipway. Lifeguards patrol from late June until early September, and dog restrictions apply from the beach access point southwards to the Carreg-y-Ddafad rocks from 1 May until 30 September.

Penbryn Beach

GRID REF **SN 292525**
GPS **52.1439°N, 4.4964°W**
COUNTY **Ceredigion**
BEACH FACES **North-west**

The National Trust's Penbryn Beach is approximately a mile long at low tide, and has a shore of sand, rocks and pebbles backed by high wooded cliffs. The pay & display car park is about 450 metres away, and has toilets, cycle stands and a cafe. From it, beach access is down a leafy lane which ends at a turning area just above the sand, enabling passengers to be dropped off. For a more scenic, yet strenuous, route, a path at the rear of the car park follows the River Hoffnant down the steep-sided, wooded Cwm Lladron or Robber's Valley.

This is a good beach for surfing and sunbathing, and is generally safe for swimming. Being largely free from light pollution, it's popular for some night-time astronomy. Dogs are not allowed from 1 May to 30 September.

Traeth Bach

GRID REF **SN 300535**
GPS **52.1531°N, 4.4852°W**
COUNTY **Ceredigion**
BEACH FACES **North-west**

Cardigan

Newport

Located approximately halfway between Llangrannog and Penbryn, Traeth Bach (Little Beach) is a secluded, sandy cove surrounded by high cliffs, with a small waterfall at the back of the beach. On the north side, the tidal island of Carreg-y-ty is pierced by a sea cave.

Access from coastal path to the beach is a short but steep descent. There are two possible routes; one leaves the coastal path at the bottom of the valley and ends with an easy scramble of about seven metres down the rocks. The slightly easier route is a steep and narrow path which leaves the coastal path on the west side, near to the field gate, and doesn't involve climbing.

Llangrannog & Cilborth

Llangrannog

GRID REF **SN 310542**
GPS **52.1597°N, 4.4710°W**
COUNTY **Ceredigion**
BEACH FACES **North-west**

Cardigan

Newport

The village of Llangrannog nestles in a steep-sided valley on the Ceredigion coast. The main beach, Traeth y Pentref, is of sand and some pebbles, flanked by high cliffs of shale and sandstone. The strangely shaped rock of Carreg Bica is on the north side of the shore, which the Nant Hawen stream flows across. The sandy cove of Cilborth is just around the point, and is also accessible from the coastal path via very steep steps.

Beach facilities include toilets, cafes, two pubs and a general store. An attended car park is situated behind the beach and a further free car park about half a mile away on the B4334, at grid ref: SN 316539 (GPS: 52.1575°N, 4.4637°W). Lifeguards patrol from the end of May until early September, and dog restrictions apply on the southern part of the beach between Nant Hawen and Pen Rhip from 1 May to 30 September. Llangrannog is a popular surfing beach, best visited between low and mid tide, but it can get crowded, and rocks and rips also pose a hazard.

Traeth yr Ysglan & Traeth y Bilis

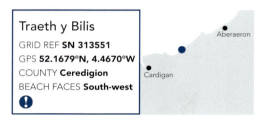

Traeth y Bilis

GRID REF **SN 313551**
GPS **52.1679°N, 4.4670°W**
COUNTY **Ceredigion**
BEACH FACES **South-west**

Tucked away beneath the headland of Lochtyn, the pristine, sandy cove of Traeth y Bilis is relatively easy to reach, although it doesn't appear so from the coastal path. It is best to visit this beach at low tide, otherwise you

might find it underwater! Access involves some minor scrambling down the headland on the north side, and needs to be done with care as there is considerable loose slate material. The beach is of clean sand with sea stacks, and the surrounding cliffs give good shelter.

Traeth yr Ysglan is 200 metres to the west, and can only be reached on foot at low tide from neighbouring Cilborth Beach, but this will usually involve a short wade around the point. Alternatively, it could be reached by a 200-metre swim from Traeth y Bilis. Parking for both beaches is as for Llangrannog.

Traeth-yr-ynys

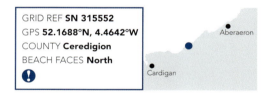

GRID REF **SN 315552**
GPS **52.1688°N, 4.4642°W**
COUNTY **Ceredigion**
BEACH FACES **North**

Situated in a particularly hilly part of Ceredigion, Traeth-yr-ynys (pronounced 'Try-thurunn- iss') is a quarter-of-a-mile-long beach of sand, rocks and small caves. Behind it is the 200-metre hill of Pen y Badell. North-facing and backed by high cliffs, it doesn't get much sun.

A steep path with some concrete steps descends to the beach from the headland,

with the last few metres a scramble down the rocks. Further out along the headland, another steep path descends to the shore, providing low-tide access to the tidal island of Ynys Lochtyn. This path begins about twenty metres from the end of the headland on the eastern side, and can be difficult to locate if you don't know where to look.

To get here from Llangrannog, one way would be to take the coastal path, but if using the car park on the B4334 (see Llangrannog), take the narrow lane which forks off to the right, about a hundred metres after crossing the stream, and follow it through Lochtyn Farm and on to the coastal path. This avoids some of the steep climbs.

Traeth Cefncwrt & Traeth Glangraig

Traeth Glangraig

GRID REF **SN 327552**
GPS **52.1692°N, 4.4466°W**
COUNTY **Ceredigion**
BEACH FACES **North**

Aberaeron

Cardigan

Traeth Glangraig, or Sea Stack Beach, is a small cove of slate rocks, shingle, sea stacks and a waterfall which tumbles down from the very top of the cliffs. The high cliffs that back the shore mean this north-facing beach doesn't get much sun.

Access is from the coastal path on the eastern side, and involves a steep descent down a gully, followed by a careful scramble down loose scree at the bottom. The cove on the far west side is Traeth Cefncwrt.

Cwmtydu

GRID REF **SN 355576**
GPS **52.1916°N, 4.4069°W**
COUNTY **Ceredigion**
BEACH FACES **North-west**

Aberaeron

Cardigan

Once the haunt of smugglers, the small cove of Cwmtydu is now owned by the National Trust. The shore is of coarse sand and shingle backed by a concrete sea wall, with the Afon Ffynnon-Ddewi emerging on the south side. At low tide, there are rock pools and caves. Free roadside parking overlooks the beach, and facilities include toilets, cycle stands and a cafe. Dogs are not allowed between 1 May and 30 September.

Castell Bach

GRID REF **SN 362583**
GPS **52.1985°N, 4.3982°W**
COUNTY **Ceredigion**
BEACH FACES **North-west**

Castell Bach is a small L-shaped beach, just north of Cwmtydu. The shore is of coarse sand and shingle flanked by mudstone cliffs, with two small islets. Once the site of an Iron Age settlement, the plateau behind the beach is now a good place to stop for a break and take in the views.

Access to the shore is a steep, rugged path at the north-west corner, and parking is available at Cwmtydu. Alternatively, roadside parking can be found on the road to St Tysilio's Church, at grid ref: SN 363573 (GPS: 52.1898°N, 4.3963°W). To get there from the latter, continue on foot to the end of the lane taking the footpath on the left through a short field to a track. Turn right, then left at the fork. Continue into the field ahead, looking for a kissing gate on the right. This leads on to the coastal path, by which time the beach will have come into view.

Traeth Soden

GRID REF **SN 362583**
GPS **52.1981°N, 4.3970°W**
COUNTY **Ceredigion**
BEACH FACES **North-west**

Traeth Soden, also known as Cwm Silio, is a peaceful, secluded cove similar to nearby Cwmtydu, but without the road. The shore is of coarse sand and shingle, backed by the deep Afon Soden valley. For approximately an hour either side of low tide, a secret cove just to the north is accessible.

Parking is available at Cwmtydu, or slightly nearer roadside parking can be found on the road to St Tysilio's Church at grid ref: SN 363573 (GPS: 52.1898°N, 4.3963°W). From the lane, take the public footpath through the churchyard and to the east side of the church. This descends into a secluded valley of ancient woodland, crossing two lively streams with waterfalls nearby. Continue across the valley to meet a path running along the valley side, which can then be followed to the beach.

1 Traeth y Coubal   **2** New Quay Harbour   **3** Dolau Beach

Traeth y Coubal

GRID REF **SN 372593**
GPS **52.2074°N, 4.3829°W**
COUNTY **Ceredigion**
BEACH FACES **West**

Traeth y Coubal is a secluded beach about a mile west of New Quay, the peace of which is only spoilt by commentary from the boat trips passing just offshore. The shore is comprised of coarse sand, pebbles and rocks, backed by high cliffs of mudstone and shale. It can be reached by one of two footpaths from the nearby lane, but the closest parking is at New Quay's Church Road (A486) car park, at grid ref: SN 386599 (GPS: 52.2134°N, 4.3632°W).

It's a secret surf spot, best around mid tide and usually empty due to the difficult access. Enjoy, but make sure you know where the rocks are!

Dolau & New Quay Harbour

Dolau

GRID REF **SN 389601**
GPS **52.2151°N, 4.3584°W**
COUNTY **Ceredigion**
BEACH FACES **East**

New Quay Harbour

GRID REF **SN 390600**
GPS **52.2142°N, 4.3569°W**
COUNTY **Ceredigion**
BEACH FACES **East**

Dolau Beach lies west of the harbour at New Quay, and is a beach of coarse sand and shells approximately 110 metres wide. Two pay & display car parks are just behind the beach, and New Quay's large Church Road car park is about 350 metres away.

East of the harbour, New Quay's sandy Harbour Beach is patrolled by lifeguards from the end of May until early September. A swimming zone is usually set up, but at some stages of the tide boats need to cross this to reach their moorings. A dog ban operates on this beach from May to September inclusive. Facilities at New Quay include toilets, numerous food outlets, pubs, beach shops, drinking water, a seasonal Tourist Information Centre and cycle parking.

Traeth Gwyn (Llanina Beach)

GRID REF **SN 396596**
GPS **52.2108°N, 4.3479°W**
COUNTY **Ceredigion**
BEACH FACES **North**

Traeth Gwyn, also known as Llanina Beach, is a crescent-shaped beach about a mile long,

located between New Quay Harbour and Llanina Point. The shore is of coarse sand and some shingle, backed by banks of boulder clay which are suffering badly from erosion. A small but free car parking area can be found at Llanina woods, at grid ref: SN 405596 (GPS: 52.2119°N, 4.3358°W), from where the coastal path leads out to the point. Swimming is generally safe.

Cei Bach

GRID REF **SN 408598**
GPS **52.2129°N, 4.3304°W**
COUNTY **Ceredigion**
BEACH FACES **North**

Cei Bach, or Little Quay, is a quiet bay east of New Quay's Traeth Gwyn Beach. About half a mile long, the shore is of coarse sand

interspersed with wooden groynes and backed by densely wooded boulder clay slopes. The road to the beach ends at a barrier, with toilets nearby. After the barrier, the lane continues for about a hundred metres to a slipway on to the sand.

A small, free parking area is at Llanina woods (see Traeth Gwyn), from where the coastal path leads to Llanina Point at the western end of the beach.

Gilfach-yr-Halen

GRID REF **SN 435614**
GPS **52.2281°N, 4.2917°W**
COUNTY **Ceredigion**
BEACH FACES **North-west**

Gilfach-yr-Halen is one of the least appealing of all Ceredigion's beaches. Situated below the

Gilfach Holiday Village, the shore consists of rocks, shingle and small patches of coarse sand, and is backed by unstable boulder clay cliffs.

From the village of Llwyncelyn on the A487, a narrow lane leads to and through the holiday village, crossing a small stream at the bottom of the valley. A stony track forks off here and leads down to the shore. Some limited space for roadside parking is available under the trees, but care must be taken not to cause obstruction.

1 Aberaeron, looking towards New Quay **2** Aberaeron, North Beach **3** Aberaeron

Aberaeron

GRID REF **SN 453629**
GPS **52.2421°N, 4.2660°W**
COUNTY **Ceredigion**
BEACH FACES **North-west**

The Georgian town of Aberaeron has two beaches: one on either side of the harbour. The south beach is the better, consisting of coarse sand at low tide backed by a pebble bank. The north beach is rocky with very little sand. In both directions from Aberaeron, the shore becomes rockier.

Dog restrictions apply on the south beach between the first groyne to south of Beach Parade and the harbour walls, from 1 May to 30 September. Pay & display parking areas overlook the beaches, and further free parking is available in the town on the north side of the harbour. Surf conditions are best between low and mid tide, but it can get crowded.

The town caters well for the summer influx of visitors and has good facilities, including a Tourist Information Centre, toilets, a supermarket, craft shops and plenty of cafes, restaurants and pubs.

Aberarth

GRID REF **SN 477639**
GPS **52.2517°N, 4.2314°W**
COUNTY **Ceredigion**
BEACH FACES **North-west**

At the tiny village of Aberarth, the Afon Arth enters the sea over a beach consisting of pebbles, shingle and some patches of coarse sand. The shore is backed by low cliffs of boulder clay, with groynes and other sea defences in place to reduce erosion. The sandiest area is south of the river, and at low tide the stone remains of fish traps can be seen.

Aberarth village is well kept, with narrow lanes and no specific parking areas, but roadside parking can be found. Probably the best place to look is on the roads leading west from the A487 south of the river bridge. There are no toilets or any other facilities, however for surfers this is a beach break at its best around mid to high tide. Hazards include rips and rocks, so it's not suitable for beginners.

Morfa Mawr

GRID REF **SN 499658**
GPS **52.2694°N, 4.2000°W**
COUNTY **Ceredigion**
BEACH FACES **West**

The beach at Morfa Mawr consists of sand, rocks, streams and rock pools, backed by banks of boulder clay which are suffering from erosion. To the south, the banks rise steeply to the shale cliffs of Graig Ddu, where the shore becomes rocky and the remains of fish traps can be seen at low tide.

Access from the A487 is by a public footpath through Morfa Mawr farm, or alternatively take the coastal path from Llanon. This stretch of coast is good for surfing, working best around mid to high tide with a small swell but watch out for rips and rocks.

Llanon & Llansantffraid

Llanon	
GRID REF **SN 506667**	
GPS **52.2777°N, 4.1902°W**	
COUNTY **Ceredigion**	
BEACH FACES **West**	
P	

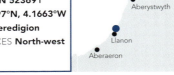

Llanon has a beach of shingle and patches of low-tide sand, backed by low boulder clay cliffs and the coastal path. The turning of Heol-y-Mor,

off the main A487 on the south of Llanon village, leads to a small parking area behind the beach. Further parking is available in the village, which has a free short-stay car park, toilets, a pub, a fish & chip shop and a store. Signposted public footpaths lead from the village to the beach.

Further north, Llansantffraid Beach can be reached by following the Stryd-yr-Eglwys lane to the church and alongside the Afon Peris, but parking nearby is difficult. As the coastal path runs further inland this is similar but more secluded than Llanon.

Llanrhystud

GRID REF **SN 523691**	
GPS **52.2997°N, 4.1663°W**	
COUNTY **Ceredigion**	
BEACH FACES **North-west**	
P 🌀	

Llanrhystud has a half-mile-long beach of low-tide sand, backed by a storm bank of shingle. The coastal path runs along the top of the shingle bank, which has been levelled to provide a reasonable walking surface. Swimming is generally safe.

South of Llanrhystud, the shore becomes

rockier, with five historic lime kilns alongside the coastal path. To the north is the Afon Wyre, beyond which the shore is completely rocky. A singletrack road from the A487 south of the petrol station leads to a small free parking area overlooking the shore.

For spending a summer's evening, a late swim, a barbecue or just to sit and watch the sun go down, this is an idyllic beach. Just a short distance from the A487, it's also a good place to stop off for a break if travelling from North to South Wales or vice-versa. Facilities at Llanrhystud village include a pub, cafe, supermarket, post office and campsite.

Morfa Bychan

GRID REF **SN 563770**
GPS **2.3717°N, 4.1111°W**
COUNTY **Ceredigion**
BEACH FACES **West**

Morfa Bychan is a beach of rocks and shingle situated below the Morfa Bychan Holiday Park. Backed by cliffs of shale and boulder clay, it has a small sandy area to the south, but the lower shore is mostly seaweed-covered rocks. In some places the unstable cliffs are overhanging and look ready to crash on to the shore at any moment. For those seeking solitude, a walk of about a mile further south along the shore will find a sandy beach which is usually deserted.

The only way on to the beach on this part of the coast is from the holiday park, where access is by means of wide wooden steps. Southwards, there is no access to the shore until five miles away at Llanrhystud, although gullies carved by small streams could provide egress in an emergency.

The Morfa Bychan Holiday Park may allow parking at their reception area for non-residents provided they are notified about the vehicle. Also, parking at the top of the hill before the gates is possible, but care must be taken not to cause obstruction.

2 Tanybwlch Beach   3 Tanybwlch Beach, beach level

Tanybwlch Beach

GRID REF **SN 579805**
GPS **52.4036°N, 4.0891°W**
COUNTY **Ceredigion**
BEACH FACES **West**

Tanybwlch's three-quarters-of-a-mile-long beach of coarse, grey, gravelly sand is backed by a substantial shingle bank which has blocked the valley behind, forcing the mouth of the Ystwyth river northwards. The shingle bank is now a Nature Reserve and carries the coastal path. Overlooking the beach is the Iron Age hill fort of Pen Dinas, which is topped by a monument in the shape of an upturned cannon.

South of Tanybwlch Beach the shore becomes rocky, and is backed by high shale cliffs. Parking is at a small, free car park at the northern end. If travelling from the south, this can be reached without having to negotiate the roads of Aberystwyth's town centre. There are no beach facilities, but Aberystwyth town is just a twenty-minute walk away.

1 Aberystwyth South, the beach from the castle end   2 Aberystwyth South

Aberystwyth South

GRID REF **SN 578813**
GPS **52.4108°N, 4.0909°W**
COUNTY **Ceredigion**
BEACH FACES **West**

●Tywyn

● Borth

● Aberystwyth

Aberystwyth South Beach reaches from the harbour wall at the southern end to the castle at the northern. Backed by a promenade, its facilities include a pay & display car park, cycle stands, toilets and showers. The upper shore is of coarse grey, gravelly sand with finer sand lower down. Aberystwyth's main town and railway station are just a short walk away, and fishing trips operate from the harbour in the summer. Dog restrictions apply between Castle Headland and the first groyne at the end of South Marine Terrace from 1 May to 30 September, and RNLI lifeguards patrol during the school summer holidays.

Surfers will find a good reef break known as the Harbour Trap at the southern end of the beach. This works best between low and mid tide with an offshore wind, but it can get busy. The rivers Rheidol and Ystwyth emerge here and can cause rips.

Aberystwyth North

GRID REF **SN 582820**
GPS **52.4172°N, 4.0853°W**
COUNTY **Ceredigion**
BEACH FACES **West**

Aberystwyth's North Beach reaches from Constitution Hill at its northern end to the town's Victorian pier at the southern end. The sand on the upper shore is grey and gravelly, becoming finer lower down, but the beach becomes rocky at either end. A dog ban operates between the north side of the landing stage and the extreme northern end of the beach from 1 May to 30 September. RNLI lifeguards patrol from mid June until early September.

Facilities include cafes, toilets, showers, drinking water, pubs, shops, a children's paddling pool and a Tourist Information Centre, with car parks and roadside parking available in the town. Aberystwyth Railway Station is 350 metres away, and is the terminus of both the Cambrian Coast line and the Vale of Rheidol line.

At the beach's northern end, Constitution Hill rises to ninety-seven metres and has a cafe, a camera obscura and extensive views of Cardigan Bay. Ascent can be made either on foot or by cliff railway.

1 Clarach Bay   **2** Wallog   **3** Aberwennol

Clarach Bay

GRID REF **SN 586838**
GPS **52.4334°N, 4.0802°W**
COUNTY **Ceredigion**
BEACH FACES **West**

Clarach Bay is just over a mile north of Aberystwyth, looking out across Cardigan Bay. The shore is comprised of coarse sand and shingle, flanked by shale cliffs. Hundreds of caravans and chalets populate the holiday parks behind the bay. The Afon Clarach emerges on the north side, next to a small, free parking area which overlooks the shore. Facilities include toilets, takeaways, cafes and a bar. Lifeguards patrol during the school summer holidays, and dog restrictions apply from 1 May to 30 September.

Wallog

GRID REF **SN 589858**
GPS **52.4515°N, 4.0766°W**
COUNTY **Ceredigion**
BEACH FACES **West**

Wallog is a remote beach in Cardigan Bay between Aberystwyth and Borth. The shore is coarse sand, shingle and rocks, flanked by shale cliffs, and behind the beach is a level grassed area and an old lime kiln. The most interesting feature of the beach is the Sarn Cynfelin – a deposit of glacial moraine which stretches for miles out under the sea. Access is via the mile-long walk along the coastal path, or alternatively by a three-quarters-of-a-mile walk along a public footpath from the B4272, but parking nearby is difficult.

Aberwennol

GRID REF **SN 600883**
GPS **52.4742°N, 4.0615°W**
COUNTY **Ceredigion**
BEACH FACES **West**

On the other side of the war memorial which tops the headland to the south of Borth resides the small cove of Aberwennol – a rocky beach with some small patches of sand, backed by unstable shale cliffs. Signs warn of crumbling cliffs and submerged objects in the water. Access is from the coastal path which drops down to near beach level.

Borth

GRID REF **SN 606898**
GPS **52.4879°N, 4.0533°W**
COUNTY **Ceredigion**
BEACH FACES **West**

The village of Borth is about a mile and a half long, built along the B4353 on a strip of land between the sea and the Cors Fochno bog. Sandy at low tide, the beach is backed by shingle and a concrete sea wall. At the southern end are the cliffs of Craig-yr-Wylfa,

where the shore becomes rockier with plenty of rock pools. On a low tide, the remains of a submerged forest are revealed.

Facilities include drinking water, toilets, hotels, cafes, shops, a free car park, a slipway and a railway station. The northern end of the beach has groynes at regular intervals and plenty of space for parking between the sea wall and the road. It's a good surfing beach up as far as Ynyslas, best around the high tide and generally suitable for beginners. Lifeguards patrol from early July until early September and dog restrictions apply from May to September on most of the southern part of the beach.

Ynyslas

GRID REF **SN 604925**
GPS **52.5121°N, 4.0574°W**
COUNTY **Ceredigion**
BEACH FACES **West**

Ynyslas (pronounced 'Unnisslass') is a beach of low-tide sand backed by a shingle bank, with dunes to the north and a golf course to the south. There are wooden sea defences in the form of groynes and a barrier along the top of the shingle bank. Parking is at an attended car park.

3 Estuary Beach

Ynyslas – Estuary Beach

GRID REF **SN 612945**
GPS **52.5302°N, 4.0464°W**
COUNTY **Ceredigion**
BEACH FACES **North-east**
🅿 🌐

Tywyn
Borth
Aberystwyth

Backed by low dunes, Ynyslas's sandy estuary beach lies on the south side of the Dyfi, opposite Aberdyfi. Parking is on the sand, but vehicles need to stay at the top of the beach where the sand is firm enough to drive on. A small fee is charged in summer, but tickets can be obtained from the nearby visitor centre, which has toilets.

Swimming is dangerous due to estuarial currents, and is not allowed. Launching of boats is also prohibited. The dunes are part of the Dyfi National Nature Reserve, and bee and marsh orchids can be seen in summer. There are also adders, so it's advisable to keep to the paths. Jutting out into the Dyfi estuary is North Point, an excellent location for shell collecting. Likely finds include smooth clams, Iceland cyprina and Faroe sunset shells. Occasionally ordnance is also found – anything suspicious should be reported to the coastguard. Ynyslas's west-facing beach is a short walk around the point or across the dunes.

The old county of Meirionnydd/Merionethshire lies in the south of the new county of Gwynedd, with generally long, sandy and west-facing beaches. The main resort town is Barmouth, which is famous for its half-mile-long timber railway viaduct across the Mawddach estuary. Six miles further north is Wales's only recognised naturist beach at Morfa Dyffryn. Heading inland, the terrain soon becomes mountainous, with deep wooded valleys, lakes, plenty of campsites and the high peaks of Rhinog Fawr and Diffwys.

This county also has fairly good access; the Cambrian Coast Line railway follows the coast from Aberystwyth to Pwllheli, and has stations within walking distance of most of the beaches. Day ranger tickets are available for those who fancy some beach-hopping. Beach supervisors are on duty at the main beaches during summer, but no Gwynedd beaches have lifeguards.

MEIRION-NYDD

Opposite Portmeirion

Aberdyfi

GRID REF **SN 612957**
GPS **52.5421°N, 4.0469°W**
COUNTY **Gwynedd**
BEACH FACES **South**

● Tywyn

● Borth

●
Aberystwyth

The Victorian village of Aberdyfi (pronounced 'Abberduvvy') lies within the Snowdonia National Park on the north side of the Dyfi estuary. Its sandy beach is backed by a sea wall with low dunes to the north. The village has plenty to do, with a small harbour that hosts sailing regattas in summer, ice cream shops, takeaways, pubs, hotels, toilets, drinking water, a Tourist Information Centre and seasonal first aid.

Some free short-term roadside parking is available, while a pay & display car park accommodates longer stays. Aberdyfi Railway Station is approximately 350 metres to the north-west and Penhelig Railway Station about the same distance to the east. Popular activities include windsurfing, kayaking, waterskiing, rowing and fishing, but there can be strong currents. Dog restrictions apply on a section of the beach from 1 April until 30 September, the western boundary of which is marked by a wooden pole.

Cemetery Beach

GRID REF **SN 592969**
GPS **52.5513°N, 4.0769°W**
COUNTY **Gwynedd**
BEACH FACES **West**

● Tywyn

● Borth

●
Aberystwyth

The four miles of coast between Tywyn and Aberdyfi is sandy and backed by low dunes.

On the A493, a mile and a half north-west of Aberdyfi, parking can be found at a long lay-by on the west side of the road opposite a cemetery, at grid ref: SN 596971 (GPS: 52.5543°N, 4.0714°W), with additional space further north on the opposite side. From here a public footpath crosses the railway, golf links and dunes to the beach, which has become known as Cemetery Beach due to its location. Swimming is generally safe.

Tywyn

GRID REF **SH 577002**
GPS **52.5806°N, 4.1004°W**
COUNTY **Gwynedd**
BEACH FACES **West**

Tywyn's long, sandy beach is interspersed with groynes. There is plenty of free parking along the promenade which backs the beach, and other facilities include takeaways, toilets, ice cream vendors, a children's paddling pool and a recreation ground with tennis courts. The town has a selection of shops and pubs, as well as a railway station a third of a mile from the beach. The narrow gauge Talyllyn Railway has its terminus here, and follows the Afon Fathew valley seven miles inland to Abergynolwyn.

The surf conditions here are good for beginners, and best south of the slipway just after the high tide. A dog ban operates for half a mile from 1 April to 30 September.

Tonfanau

GRID REF **SH 560033**
GPS **52.6080°N, 4.1268°W**
COUNTY **Gwynedd**
BEACH FACES **West**

Tonfanau (pronounced 'Tonnvan-eye') is a little-visited beach of sand and rocks, backed by shingle and boulder clay banks. The Afon Dysynni emerges to the south, while northwards the shore is mostly rocks, shingle and some low-tide sandy areas.

Tonfanau Railway Station is approximately a quarter of a mile away, and access to the shore is along a public footpath, passing the remains of an old army camp. The adjacent road is relatively wide with little traffic, and roadside parking is possible near the station.

Cae-Du

GRID REF **SH 566060**
GPS **52.6324°N, 4.1192°W**
COUNTY **Gwynedd**
BEACH FACES **West**

The shore at Cae-Du (pronounced 'Kiy-dee') is a mix of rocks and patches of low-tide sand, backed by boulder clay cliffs, a campsite and the Cambrian Coast Line railway. Parking can also be found in lay-bys half a mile north on the A493, but be aware that the county road ends at the railway bridge; there is no public right of way on to the shore.

Llwyngwril

GRID REF **SH 588101**
GPS **52.6698°N, 4.0884°W**
COUNTY **Gwynedd**
BEACH FACES **North-west**

Llwyngwril, which is is pronounced 'Hlwin-goo-ril' and translates as 'Grove of Green Leaves', is a beach of rocks and some low-tide sand, backed by a pebble bank with some sandy areas to the north. A small, free car park with seasonal toilets is located just off the A493

(follow signs for the station). Access to the shore from here is along the lane, crossing the Afon Gwril just before the railway, and continuing along a tarmac footpath on the north side of the river. Llwyngwril Railway Station is approximately 300 metres from the beach and the car park about 450 metres. The beach has no facilities, but the village has a pub and a small shop.

The surf here is unreliable but can be good with a southwesterly wind, and is usually best around high tide. Rocks can be a hazard and it's not a beach for the inexperienced.

Fairbourne & Morfa Mawddach

Fairbourne
GRID REF **SH 610130**
GPS **52.6964°N, 4.0571°W**
COUNTY **Gwynedd**
BEACH FACES **West**

Fairbourne's two-mile sandy beach is backed by a pebble bank to the south and low dunes to the north, and extends as a spit into the Mawddach estuary. Swimming is generally safe at the beach's centre, but there can be currents near the river. Car parks are conveniently located at the centre of the beach and at either end, and toilets and drinking water are available. However, dog restrictions apply to the southern half of the beach from 1 April to 30 September.

Stations for the Cambrian Coast Line and the narrow gauge Fairbourne Railway are a level walk of half a mile away. The latter runs to the beach's northern end, usually connecting with a passenger ferry to Barmouth.

Morfa Mawddach beach lies between the Fairbourne spit and Barmouth Bridge on the southern side of the Mawddach estuary. A wide expanse of soft sand backed by very low dunes, it can be reached by following a foot or cyclepath from Morfa Mawddach station towards the bridge, where a stile on the right gives access to the shore. Parking and toilets can be found at the station, formerly a junction with a branch line to Ruabon.

A cyclepath known as the Mawddach Trail follows this route for seven miles inland to Dolgellau.

Barmouth

GRID REF **SH 611155**
GPS **52.7189°N, 4.0567°W**
COUNTY **Gwynedd**
BEACH FACES **South-west**

The popular seaside town of Barmouth lies within Snowdonia National Park, on the north side of the Mawddach estuary. The wide estuary is crossed by a half-mile-long timber railway bridge, which has a footpath/cyclepath alongside the railway track.

Barmouth's main beach is backed by low dunes and a promenade, and is subject to a dog ban from 1 April to 30 September. A beach supervisor is on duty during the summer, but watch out for sandbars and fast currents near the estuary.

Nearby facilities include deckchair hire, toilets, drinking water, a slipway, fairground rides, cafes and plenty of pay & display parking. The town centre has more shops, cafes, hotels, a supermarket, a Tourist Information Centre and a railway station, which is 100 metres from the beach. North of the town the shore is backed by shingle, and a further large car park is available at this end, but Barmouth's streets are very narrow and traffic congestion is likely on busy days. Parking at a nearby local station and taking the train, which departs every two hours, can be a good option.

Surf conditions are consistently good at any stage of the tide, and the fact that it rarely gets crowded makes it even better. Panoramic views of the town and estuary can be seen from the National Trust property of Dinas Oleu, which can be reached by going up a steep zigzagging path via Dinas Oleu Road.

Llanaber

GRID REF **SH 598181**
GPS **52.7419°N, 4.0771°W**
COUNTY **Gwynedd**
BEACH FACES **West**

The small village of Llanaber has a sandy beach backed by a sea wall which protects the railway. Some lay-by parking is available on the A496 outside a cemetery, from which access to the shore is by one of two footpaths. The first of these leaves the road south of the cemetery, crosses the railway by a footbridge and continues south between the railway and a sea defence wall of boulders. The better option, which is signposted to Llanaber station, crosses the railway and leads to a ramp down to the shore. As the tide comes right up to the sea wall, however, access to the beach from Llanaber is only possible around low tide.

Tal-y-bont

GRID REF **SH 578211**
GPS **52.7684°N, 4.1080°W**
COUNTY **Gwynedd**
BEACH FACES **South-west**

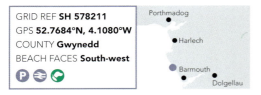

The small village of Tal-y-bont on the A496 has a long beach of sand, backed by shingle, dunes and campsites. There is no proper car park here, but a road, Fford Glan Y Môr, leads from the village to the shore and is amply wide enough for roadside parking. A nearby campsite has a supermarket, pub and shop, and Tal-y-bont Railway Station is about half a mile away.

Bennar

GRID REF **SH 568226**
GPS **52.7816°N, 4.1234°W**
COUNTY **Gwynedd**
BEACH FACES **South-west**

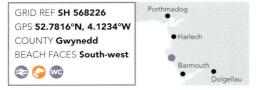

Bennar's long, sandy beach is backed by a pebble bank and dunes. A landscaped pay & display car park is approximately 200 metres away, and access to the shore is a boardwalk over the dunes. Facilities on this beach include toilets, a picnic area and two campsites. The nearest railway station, Dyffryn Ardudwy, is approximately a mile away, adjacent to a pub. Dog restrictions operate to the south of the main access point for about 900 metres to the Afon Ysgethin, from 1 April to 30 September.

Morfa Dyffryn

GRID REF **SH 563233**
GPS **52.7877°N, 4.1311°W**
COUNTY **Gwynedd**
BEACH FACES **South-west**

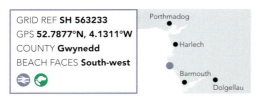

begins approximately half a mile north of the main access point and continues northwards for another half a mile.

Aside from this, swimming is generally safe. Behind the dunes is a holiday park with a grass parking area. This is attended during busy periods. To get here, take the road for Bennar Beach from the A496 and turn right half a mile after the level crossing. From the car park, access to the beach is a 200-metre walk across the dunes. Dyffryn Ardudwy Railway Station is one mile away.

Backed by some impressive dunes, the long sandy beach of Morfa Dyffryn is known for being an officially recognised naturist beach. The area set aside for this, marked by signs,

1 Shell Island, the beach below the campsite   **2** Shell Island, dunes to the south   **3** Llandanwg   **4** Llandanwg, the harbour

Shell Island (Mochras)

GRID REF **SH 550260**
GPS **52.8116°N, 4.1516°W**
COUNTY **Gwynedd**
BEACH FACES **West**

Shell Island is home to one of the largest campsites in Europe, with some 300 acres of camping space for tents only. Parking for day visitors is usually allowed, and the site can be

reached across a causeway from Llanbedr which occasionally floods on high tides, although access on foot from the south is always possible. Be sure to check the cut-off times.

The shore varies from rocky to sandy, with high sand dunes to the south. Although this is the best area for bathing there are other smaller sandy areas. A good destination for shell collectors, it is claimed that 200 different varieties of shells have been found here. Facilities include toilets, a bar and a supermarket.

Llandanwg

GRID REF **SH 566283**
GPS **52.8327°N, 4.1289°W**
COUNTY **Gwynedd**
BEACH FACES **North-west**

The coarse, pebbly sand of Llandanwg is backed by low dunes, with a sandy harbour protected by a concrete breakwater at the southern end. Although it's generally safe for swimming, rip currents can occur in surf

conditions. As with nearby Shell Island, a good variety of seashells can be found here.

Dog restrictions apply to the left of the main access for 300 metres between 1 April and 30 September. A small pay & display car park with additional roadside parking is available nearby, and access to the beach is along a short path. Adjacent to this car park is the small St Tanwg's church, which is seemingly in danger of being engulfed by the dunes! Facilities include toilets, drinking water and a cafe, and Llandanwg Railway Station is 350 metres away.

Harlech

GRID REF **SH 568316**
GPS **52.8624°N, 4.1274°W**
COUNTY **Gwynedd**
BEACH FACES **South-west**

Porthmadog
Harlech
Barmouth
Dolgellau

Known for its heavily fortified medieval castle, the village of Harlech has a four-mile sandy beach backed by dunes and a golf course. To the north is the Glaslyn estuary, where strong currents can occur, but away from this end bathing is generally safe.

Parking is at a pay & display car park, which has seasonal toilets, cycle parking and usually refreshment vans in summer. Dog restrictions apply north of the main access point for a distance of about 450 metres, from 1 April until 30 September. Beach access is a tarmac path which leads 350 metres across the dunes. Harlech's railway station and swimming pool are both about half a mile away.

3 Ynys Gifftan, the west side of the island   **4** Ynys Gifftan, the east side

Ynys Gifftan

GRID REF **SH 600368**
GPS **52.9100°N, 4.0821°W**
COUNTY **Gwynedd**
BEACH FACES **South**

Ynys Gifftan is a small, privately owned tidal island in the wide Afon Dwyryd estuary, near the village of Talsarnau. Roughly circular, it's covered in bracken and scrub with a derelict cottage on the eastern side. The shore on most sides is sandy with a few rock pools, and access is a public footpath from Talsarnau Railway Station, which leads across marshy pasture and the sands of the estuary. As with most tidal crossings this one comes with the usual warnings, but the island is only about 350 metres from the shore and is only cut off for a short time around high tide. However, on such a wide estuary with little gradient, the sand will flood quickly on a rising tide. If crossing be aware of the state of the tide, and look out for any channels in the sand which could fill early.

Llandecwyn

GRID REF **SH 619383**
GPS **52.9240°N, 4.0545°W**
COUNTY **Gwynedd**
BEACH FACES **South**

At Llandecwyn, the Afon Dwyryd is crossed by the combined rail and road bridge of Pont Briwet, and the sandy estuary has dramatic views towards the Moelwyn mountains. Access is a public footpath from Pont Briwet, which follows the eastern side of the river. Some space for roadside parking is available, but care must be taken not to cause obstruction. Alternatively, Llandecwyn Railway Station is just 100 metres away.

Abergafren

GRID REF **SH 600379**
GPS **52.9199°N, 4.0826°W**
COUNTY **Gwynedd**
BEACH FACES **East**

A narrow lane from the A497 at Minffordd, initially signposted for Portmeirion, leads to a small parking area overlooking the sandy Afon Dwyryd estuary. Just to the north is a cove, while to the immediate south the sandy shore is backed by a small area of salt marsh. If you look out from the centre of the estuary you will see the tidal island of Ynys Gifftan.

Something to bear in mind is that the sand has very little gradient, so will flood quickly on a rising tide. Signs warn that swimming is dangerous due to currents.

Portmeirion

GRID REF **SH 587367**
GPS **52.9088°N, 4.1014°W**
COUNTY **Gwynedd**
BEACH FACES **South-east**

Portmeirion is a popular Italian-style tourist village created by Sir Bertram Clough Williams-Ellis. Its beach consists of soft sand backed by low cliffs. Plenty of nooks and crannies offer shelter for sunbathing, but swimming is not advisable due to estuarial currents, and most of the sand is covered at high tide.

Access to the shore is through the village, which charges an entrance fee. However, this beach is open daily and has plenty of car parking, toilets, cafes and shops. Dogs are not allowed in Portmeirion village. The closest railway station is Minffordd, a mile and a half away.

The Llŷn Peninsula in the county of Gwynedd juts out into the Irish Sea. The beaches along its southern shore are mostly long and sandy, while the northern coast up as far as Porthdinllaen is indented with numerous secret coves and smaller sandy beaches. North of Porthdinllaen the beaches become longer, and a colourful variety of pebbles can be found on the shores, including white quartz pebbles, red jasper and purple slates. The western tip of the Llŷn Peninsula is an area of winding lanes, good footpaths and plenty of campsites, but very few shops or cafes. No Gwynedd beaches have lifeguards.

THE LLŶN PENINSULA & SNOWDONIA

1 **Traeth Mawr,** from the Cob 2 **Traeth Mawr,** on the tideline looking towards Porthmadog

Traeth Mawr (Porthmadog)

GRID REF **SH 575380**
GPS **52.9201°N, 4.1198°W**
COUNTY **Gwynedd**
BEACH FACES **South**

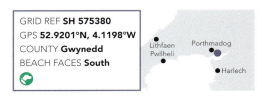

Porthmadog Cob was built to carry the Ffestiniog Railway across the wide Afon Glaslyn estuary and to reclaim a large area of low-lying land to the north. The shore to the south is essentially a large sandbank with a few muddy bits, turning to salt marsh towards the north-eastern corner.

The sandy shore has very little gradient and will flood quickly on a rising tide. As with most sandbanks, there are numerous channels which will fill early, so a close eye needs to be kept on the tide if you want to visit this beach and leave without getting wet.

On the west side is the artificial island of Cei Ballast, built up over the years from ballast dumped by the ships returning to Porthmadog. Few people come here, and access to the shore is from the Cob, where a footpath runs alongside the railway. Low-tide access is also possible along the shore from Portmeirion.

3 Borth-y-Gest   **4** Borth-y-Gest, first beach to the south-west

Borth-y-Gest

GRID REF **SH 565374**
GPS **52.9145°N, 4.1344°W**
COUNTY **Gwynedd**
BEACH FACES **South-east**

The Victorian village of Borth-y-Gest borders the Afon Glaslyn and looks out across Tremadog Bay towards the Rhinog mountains.

Backed by a sea wall and a crescent-shaped promenade, the upper shore is initially sand, graduating to mud lower down. Better, sandier coves can be found a short walk to the south-west. The shale cliffs which back these are indented with nooks and crannies providing shelter for sunbathing, but swimming is not advisable due to estuarial currents.

Facilities at Borth-y-Gest include a free car park and roadside parking, toilets, tearooms and a slipway.

Carreg Wen & Samson's Bay

Carreg Wen

GRID REF **SH 560370**
GPS **52.9107°N, 4.1416°W**
COUNTY **Gwynedd**
BEACH FACES **South**

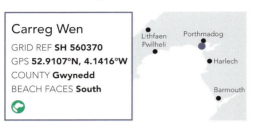

Lithfaen
Pwllheli

Porthmadog

Harlech

Barmouth

Carreg Wen is a sandy cove lying between the headlands of Fechan Point and Garreg Goch. Backed by low dunes, the 300-metre-wide bay borders the Afon Glaslyn. The nearest parking is half a mile away at Borth-y-Gest.

The next cove along is Samson's Bay; a sheltered crescent of sand backed by a sea wall of boulders, the coastal path and a golf course. Swimming is not advisable due to strong estuarial currents.

4 Black Rock Sands   **5** Black Rock Sands, from the eastern end

Black Rock Sands

GRID REF **SH 527371**
GPS **52.9107°N, 4.1907°W**
COUNTY **Gwynedd**
BEACH FACES **South-west**

Lithfaen
Pwllheli
Porthmadog
Harlech
Barmouth

Black Rock Sands is a sandy beach, reaching a mile and a half from the Glaslyn estuary to the dolerite headland of Black Rock. Parking is on the sand; two main gated access points are open from early morning to late evening in the summer. Both have seasonal toilets, and drinking water is available. At the Black Rock headland there are some caves, and the Afon Cedron emerges on to the shore. Additionally, a large sandbar known as the North Bank is at the south-eastern end of the beach.

Swimming is generally safe away from the Glaslyn estuary, which has strong currents. Occasionally the waves are big enough for surfing and the beach is extensively zoned for different activities. There are no lifeguards, but wardens patrol continuously on busy days. Dogs are not allowed between the main access point and Black Rock from 1 April until 30 September.

Criccieth

GRID REF **SH 510379**
GPS **52.9175°N, 4.2164°W**
COUNTY **Gwynedd**
BEACH FACES **South**

The thirteenth-century Criccieth Castle (pronounced 'Crickyeth') stands prominently on a headland with sandy beaches to either side. East of the village, Promenade Beach consists of sand and pebbles, backed by a sea wall. Extending to the east for about a mile towards Graig Ddu or Black Rock, this end is sandier and backed by a storm bank of pebbles and the Cambrian Coast Line railway.

At low tide, neighbouring Black Rock Sands can be reached along the shore. Roadside parking is available on the promenade, with additional pay & display parking nearby, and access to the shore is down a concrete ramp or steps. Dog restrictions apply between the harbour wall and the groyne at the end of the promenade from April to September inclusive. Facilities include an ice cream shop, toilets, drinking water and a first aid post.

Marine Beach is west of the castle, and is sandy with some shingle and interspersed groynes. Generally safe for swimming, it has plenty of roadside parking and a small free car park at the western end. Dog restrictions apply at the eastern end of this beach up as far as Queen's Road. Criccieth village has a good range of shops, pubs and cafes, as well as a railway station, all within walking distance.

Ynysgain

GRID REF **SH 485374**
GPS **52.9123°N, 4.2533°W**
COUNTY **Gwynedd**
BEACH FACES **South**

Lying to the west of Criccieth, Ynysgain has a beach of shingle and low-tide sand backed by boulder clay cliffs, with the Afon Dwyfor emerging at the western end. The nearest parking is at Criccieth's Marine Beach, from where access is via the mostly level coastal path or, tide permitting, along the shore.

Afon Wen Beach

GRID REF **SH 443370**
GPS **52.9075°N, 4.3155°W**
COUNTY **Gwynedd**
BEACH FACES **South**

Afon Wen is a wide beach of sand and shingle, backed by banks of boulder clay and some sea defence walls. Most of the beach's visitors come from the Hafan y Môr Holiday Park on the western side. The beach has a very shallow gradient, making it generally safe for swimming and paddling.

A narrow lane from the Afon Wen roundabout on the A497 leads to a bridge under the railway, and space here for both parking and turning is very limited. Beach access is then a level walk of 200 metres along a gravel path.

Porth Fechan (Hafan y Môr Beach)

GRID REF **SH 436358**
GPS **52.8965°N, 4.3271°W**
COUNTY **Gwynedd**
BEACH FACES **East**

The sheltered, sandy cove of Porth Fechan, which translates as 'small cove', lies on the eastern side of the Penychain headland. Backed by a grassy area with access from the coastal path, a similar, smaller cove can be found to the south. Despite the nearby Hafan y Môr Holiday Park there is no parking close by, but Penychain Railway Station is about one and a third miles away.

Abererch Beach

GRID REF **SH 402358**
GPS **52.8955°N, 4.3758°W**
COUNTY **Gwynedd**
BEACH FACES **South**

Holiday Centre. Westwards the sandy shore continues to Pwllheli, while the eastern end is bounded by the Penychain headland. The holiday park provides a free parking area for beach visitors just after the level crossing, though this is for cars only and has a two-metre height restriction.

Access to the beach is a level walk of 150 metres from the car park, and the beach is approximately 200 metres from Abererch Railway Station.

Behind the dunes which back the two-mile beach at Abererch is the Abererch Sands

Pwllheli Glan-y-Don

GRID REF **SH 385350**
GPS **52.8878°N, 4.4007°W**
COUNTY **Gwynedd**
BEACH FACES **East**

Glan-y-Don is Pwllheli's eastern beach. A car park sits behind the sandy shore, which has some low-tide mud towards the southern side, and access is down a wide slipway. Dog restrictions apply south of this slipway between 1 April to 30 September. For facilities make your way to Pwllheli town; three quarters of a mile away, it has a good selection of shops, cafes, pubs and supermarkets, as well as a railway station.

Pwllheli South Beach

GRID REF **SH 377341**
GPS **52.8807°N, 4.4121°W**
COUNTY **Gwynedd**
BEACH FACES **South**

Pwllheli South Beach is a long stretch of sand and small pebbles, backed by dunes and a promenade. Access to the shore is a few metres' walk across the dunes, and toilets are nearby. The dunes are home to species such as sea holly, sea rocket, sea spurge, chicory, beach rose and tree mallows. Bounding the beach at its eastern end is the dolerite outcrop of Gimblet Rock – a popular spot with local children for diving and jumping. Appropriately, the name 'Pwllheli' translates as 'salt water pool'.

Dog restrictions apply on a section of the beach between Cardiff Road and Embankment Road from 1 April to 30 September. Pwllheli town is about half a mile away along Embankment Road, which has free bays for parking and a small car park at its seaward end. Backing the beach is The Promenade, which has pay & display parking. The town centre is quite vibrant in summer, and has a good selection of shops, cafes, pubs, a supermarket, a leisure centre, as well as bus and railway stations.

Traeth Crugan

GRID REF **SH 343328**
GPS **52.8668°N, 4.4619°W**
COUNTY **Gwynedd**
BEACH FACES **South-east**

Traeth Crugan is a quiet beach of coarse sand and shingle, backed by boulder clay banks. At the western end is the headland of Carreg y Defaid, while eastwards the shore continues for two and a half miles to Pwllheli. A no through road off the A499 east of the nearby Llanbedrog leads to the coastal path and is wide enough for parking. Access to the shore is then along a short concrete path.

Llanbedrog

GRID REF **SH 331313**
GPS **52.8529°N, 4.4790°W**
COUNTY **Gwynedd**
BEACH FACES **South-east**

Lithfaen
Pwllheli

Llanbedrog's mile-long beach is well known for its picturesque row of brightly coloured beach huts. At the western end the towering granite headland of Mynydd Tir-y-Cwmwd, standing at 132 metres, shelters the bay from Atlantic swells providing generally safe conditions for swimming. The beach's eastern end is bounded by the smaller headland of Carreg y Defaid, while the upper shore is mostly coarse sand and shingle.

Lower down, a good variety of small pebbles can be found, including plenty of white quartz. Facilities at the beach include an ice cream shop, seasonal toilets and cycle parking. Parking can be found at a National Trust car park just behind the beach.

Quarry Beach & The Warren

Quarry Beach

GRID REF **SH 329302**
GPS **52.8430°N, 4.4814°W**
COUNTY **Gwynedd**
BEACH FACES **South-east**

The Warren's sandy beach is backed by low dunes and extends for a mile and a half north-east from Abersoch Harbour to the headland of Trwyn Llanbedrog. The Warren Holiday Park, which sits just behind the beach, owns part of the shore and uses it extensively for boat launching, but there are no access restrictions. The beach's eastern end is known as Quarry Beach and the far western end is known as 'Traeth Tywyn y Fach', or more simply as 'The Fach'.

Parking at the Abersoch end is available in pay & display bays alongside the A499, from where beach access is a short, sandy path through the National Trust's Tywyn y Fach property. Some free lay-by parking is available 230 metres east of the holiday park entrance, and from here beach access is a public footpath through the park. For Quarry Beach, a small car park is located just behind the shore at grid ref: SH 328303 (GPS: 52.8450°N, 4.4834°W), and can be reached via some very narrow lanes around the side of Mynydd Tir-y-Cwmwd.

Abersoch Harbour

GRID REF **SH 316283**
GPS **52.8255°N, 4.4997°W**
COUNTY **Gwynedd**
BEACH FACES **North**

Abersoch's Harbour Beach is to the east of the village and can be reached along Lon Pen Cei, but parking nearby is difficult. The Afon Soch flows across the sand, and a dog ban applies south of it from April to September inclusive. Access to the shore is down steps or a slipway.

Abersoch has a lively village centre during the summer, and a good selection of hotels, B&Bs, cafes, bars, takeaways and beach shops.

Abersoch

GRID REF **SH 317278**
GPS **52.8210°N, 4.4992°W**
COUNTY **Gwynedd**
BEACH FACES **East**

Abersoch's main sandy beach is south of the village and is backed by low dunes and beach huts. Looking out across Tremadog Bay, the Cambrian mountains provide an impressive backdrop, and the southern end of the beach is known as Machroes. Abersoch is a popular beach for watersports such as sailing, jet skiing, windsurfing and swimming, so at peak times both the shore and the sea can get crowded – even a little chaotic. However, wardens patrol during the summer and some zoning with buoys is in place to keep power crafts away from swimmers.

Parking is at one of two pay & display car parks, which can be reached via the roads Lon Traeth and Lon Golff. Access to the shore is down slipways, but dog restrictions apply from 1 April until 30 September between them. Facilities include toilets, drinking water, cold water showers, a first aid post and ice cream shops.

Machroes

GRID REF **SH 317266**
GPS **52.8103°N, 4.4973°W**
COUNTY **Gwynedd**
BEACH FACES **North-east**

Reached through the village of Bwlchtocyn, Machroes Beach is at the southern end of Abersoch's main beach. The shore is of sand and small shingle interspersed with wooden groynes and backed by low dunes. Access is down a slipway from a pay & display car park, and facilities include seasonal toilets, a cafe and a lawned area with picnic tables. As well as being ideal for shell collecting, swimming is generally safe here.

Porth Bach

GRID REF **SH 324264**
GPS **52.8087°N, 4.4868°W**
COUNTY **Gwynedd**
BEACH FACES **North-east**

Just around the Penrhyn Du headland from Machroes lies the small, sheltered cove of Porth Bach. Backed by private land, it can be reached by an easy walk or scramble around the rocky point at low tide.

Porth Ceiriad

GRID REF **SH 312248**
GPS **52.7939°N, 4.5038°W**
COUNTY **Gwynedd**
BEACH FACES **South**

Lithfaen
Pwllheli

Porth Ceiriad is set in superb scenery at the southern end of the Llŷn Peninsula. Lying between the sandstone headlands of Trwyn yr Wylfa and Trwyn Cilan, the shore is coarse sand backed by unstable cliffs of sand and boulder clay. South facing and sheltered, it's good for sunbathing and watersports, such as swimming, bodyboarding, kayaking and sailing. This is also a popular surf beach, with conditions best around mid to high tide. With a good swell the waves refract from the cliffs producing barrelling wedges, but rips can occur in surf conditions.

A car parking area at a nearby campsite overlooks the bay, and is reached along a narrow lane south of the village of Bwlchtocyn. The lane is not signposted for Porth Ceiriad but has a 'no through road' sign at its junction. This leads to the campsite, entry to which is by means of a coin-operated automatic barrier. Beach access is then a walk of 300 metres to some concrete steps. Alternative pay & display parking can be found at grid ref: SH 312253 (GPS: 52.7987°N, 4.5042°W).

Hell's Mouth (Porth Neigwl)

GRID REF **SH 282264**
GPS **52.8074°N, 4.5491°W**
COUNTY **Gwynedd**
BEACH FACES **South-west**

Lithfaen
Pwllheli

Hell's Mouth, or Porth Neigwl, is a three-and-a-half-mile-long sandy beach on the south-west side of the Llŷn Peninsula. The shore is backed by banks of sand and boulder clay, which become higher towards the north-west end. Parking is at a small, free car park with further roadside parking available nearby.

From the car park, beach access is then a 200-metre walk along a sandy path. Refreshments are available from catering and ice cream vans in summer but there are no toilets. The north-west end of the beach is quieter, and a small car parking area and roadside parking are available just off the Rhiw Road at grid ref: SH 241285 (GPS: 52.8260°N, 4.6109°W). Access to this end of the beach is a rugged path down the subsiding boulder clay cliffs.

For those looking to get out into the ocean, surf conditions are fairly consistent but best between mid and high tide. Windsurfing is also popular, but it's only for the more experienced. Rip currents occur in surf conditions and swimming can be dangerous.

Porth Llawenan & Porth Ysgo

Porth Llawenan

GRID REF **SH 213262**
GPS **52.8033°N, 4.6513°W**
COUNTY **Gwynedd**
BEACH FACES **South**

....

Porth Ysgo

GRID REF **SH 207264**
GPS **52.8049°N, 4.6603°W**
COUNTY **Gwynedd**
BEACH FACES **South**

Lithfaen
Pwllheli

found at grid ref: SH 211269 (GPS: 52.8100°N, 4.6543°W), just off the Rhiw–Aberdaron road. From here, access to the beach is a footpath along a scenic V-shaped valley, leading to a steep path with roughly 140 steps. Alternative parking can be found further along the lane at Ysgo farm. Remnants of the Nant Gadwen Manganese Mine can be seen in the valleys, including some adits which have not been blocked off.

Porth Llawenan is about 200 metres to the east and is a similar beach of sand and rocks, but the land behind it is private and it can only be reached along the rocky shore from Porth Ysgo. Between the two beaches is the tiny rocky cove of Porth Alum.

About half a mile south west of Porth Ysgo is the tidal island of Maen Gwenonwy, linked to the mainland by a shingle tombolo. The beach marked on maps as Porth Cadlan is on the east side of this, and although shown as sandy, it's actually all rocks and shingle.

Owned by the National Trust, Porth Ysgo (pronounced 'Ussgo') is a small, sheltered beach at the tip of the Llŷn Peninsula. The shore is sand and shingle, backed by high cliffs and the Pistyll y Gaseg waterfall, but very little beach is available at high tide. Limited roadside parking can be

3 Porth Simdde   **4** Aberdaron Beach, the eastern end   **5** Aberdaron Beach

Aberdaron & Porth Simdde

Aberdaron

GRID REF **SH 173263**
GPS **52.8029°N, 4.7106°W**
COUNTY **Gwynedd**
BEACH FACES **South**

Lithfaen
Pwllheli

Aberdaron's sandy bay is about one and a quarter miles long and backed by banks of boulder clay, with a concrete sea wall protecting the village. The sand tends to be coarse at the top of the beach, becoming finer lower down. Two streams, Afon Cyllyfelin and Afon Daron, flow on to the beach after merging in the village.

Parking can be found at an attended car park in the village, and facilities include seasonal toilets, cycle parking, picnic tables, a first aid post, beach shops and two pubs. Dog restrictions apply on about 140 metres of the shore near the village, from 1 April to 30 September. Popular activities include swimming, windsurfing, kayaking and surfing. Surf conditions are best around high tide and it's generally suitable for beginners, but make sure you know where the rock is!

Porth Simdde is at the western end of Aberdaron Bay, and becomes a small cove for about two hours either side of high tide. During this period it can be accessed from the coastal path which drops down to near beach level.

Porth Meudwy

GRID REF **SH 164255**
GPS **52.7954°N, 4.7251°W**
COUNTY **Gwynedd**
BEACH FACES **East**

Lithfaen
Pwllheli

Porth Meudwy, which translates as 'Hermit's Cove', is a small cove of sand and rocks, backed by high cliffs, and is the departure point for boat trips to Bardsey Island (see page 332). A free National Trust car park is pleasantly situated in a grassy hollow at grid ref: SH 159259 (GPS: 52.7993°N, 4.7319°W) about 650 metres away. From here a track descends to the beach.

Porth Llanllawen & Porthorion

Porth Llanllawen

GRID REF **SH 145265**
GPS **52.8055°N, 4.7522°W**
COUNTY **Gwynedd**
BEACH FACES **North-west**

Lithfaen
Pwllheli

Lying near the tip of the Llŷn Peninsula, Porth Llanllawen is a tiny cove of rocks and shingle,

backed by a steep valley. A stream runs across the shore and a short cave is on the north side. Access from Llanllawen village is by a public footpath which leads half a mile across fields before descending the valley behind the beach.

Porthorion, found at grid ref: SH 156288 (GPS: 52.8253°N, 4.7382°W), lies a mile and a half to the north-west, and is a tiny cove of rocks and pebbles. Access is a public footpath from nearby Capel Carmel.

Whistling Sands (Porthor)

GRID REF **SH 167306**
GPS **52.8413°N, 4.7219°W**
COUNTY **Gwynedd**
BEACH FACES **North-west**

Lithfaen
Pwllheli

At the north-west end of the Llŷn Peninsula, the sandy bay of Whistling Sands is backed by banks of sand and boulder clay. The sand itself is made up of quartz grains of a mostly uniform size, which under dry conditions make a squeaky sound when walked on, hence the beach's name.

From the coast road, a short lane leads to a National Trust car park, from where beach access is a walk of about 300 metres further down the lane, which ends in a slipway. Some roadside parking can be found at the next road junction to the north from where, a little further along, a public footpath leads to the northern end of the beach.

Facilities include a cafe and beach shop and toilets, and dogs are not allowed between 1 April and 30 September. Surf conditions can be good in winter either side of high tide and with a south-west wind, but it can get busy. Rips and a few lone rocks can be a hazard.

Porth y Wrach

GRID REF **SH 167300**
GPS **52.8359°N, 4.7216°W**
COUNTY **Gwynedd**
BEACH FACES **North-west**

Porth y Wrach is one of the northern Llŷn's more scenic beaches, though it only appears on very low tides. It's an appealing mix of sand, large rocks, caves and rock pools. The best way on to the shore involves a scramble down a steep,

grassy bank and rocks at the northern end. Once at beach level, more rocks and boulders need to be negotiated to reach the sand.

Even at the height of summer you will probably have Porth y Wrach, which translates as 'Wrasse Cove', to yourself, but keep a close eye on the incoming tide.

The nearest parking is to the north of Whistling Sands, at grid ref: SH 174302 (GPS: 52.8387°N, 4.7122°W). A public footpath links to the coastal path at the southern end of Porth y Wrach.

Porth Iago

GRID REF **SH 166316**
GPS **52.8502°N, 4.7239°W**
COUNTY **Gwynedd**
BEACH FACES **South-west**

Porth Iago (pronounced 'Yargo') is a picturesque sandy bay situated between the headlands of Dinas and Graig Ddu. The pay & display parking area overlooks the beach and is reached along a private track through Ty Mawr Farm. Final access is down a steep, sandy path. If the route through the farm is closed, proceed as for Porth Ferin and take the coastal path back around the Penrhyn Mawr headland. Dogs are allowed but must be in vehicles when passing through the farm.

Porth Ferin & Porth Bach

Porth Ferin
GRID REF **SH 172321**
GPS **52.8549°N, 4.7153°W**
COUNTY **Gwynedd**
BEACH FACES **North**

Porth Ferin is a small bay of sand and shingle backed by a steep grassy bank. To get there,

follow the lane signposted for Porth Iago to the end, and then go along the public footpath directly ahead. After passing a gate, turn right immediately after the first building to a field gate, which opens on to the coastal path overlooking Porth Ferin.

Porth Bach lies to the east of Porth Ferin, and is a cove of shingle with some low-tide sand. Access is down a wide path.

Porth Widlin

GRID REF **SH 182326**
GPS **52.8598°N, 4.7008°W**
COUNTY **Gwynedd**
BEACH FACES **North**

The remote cove of Porth Widlin lies about a mile west of Llangwnnadl on the Llŷn Peninsula, and is a beach of shingle and some low-tide sand backed by boulder clay banks.

Porth Lefesig

GRID REF **SH 185325**
GPS **52.8590°N, 4.6963°W**
COUNTY **Gwynedd**
BEACH FACES **North**
❶

Porth Lefesig (also known as Porth Fesyg) is a sheltered cove of coarse sand with rock pools to either side. Backed by steep banks, the easiest way on to the shore involves criss-crossing these to avoid the steepest parts. A public footpath leads to the beach from the lane at grid ref: SH 189320 (GPS: 52.8552°N, 4.6902°W), following the more south-westerly of the two fields. If parking in the vicinity, take care not to cause obstruction.

Porth Ty-mawr

GRID REF **SH 188331**
GPS **52.8645°N, 4.6921°W**
COUNTY **Gwynedd**
BEACH FACES **West**
❶

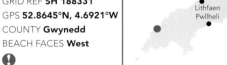

Porth Ty-mawr is a remote, sheltered beach of shingle and sand with low-tide rock pools. Backed by a steep grass bank with cliffs to the side, there are several possible routes down, all involving a bit of a scramble.

On Easter Sunday 1901, a sailing ship named the *Stuart* was wrecked here carrying whisky from Liverpool, and on a low tide its remains can be seen. Much of its cargo ended up in the hands of local villagers, some of which was buried to hide it from customs officers. Over 100 years later, bottles are still being discovered.

1 Porth Ty-llwyd   **2** Porth Colmon   **3** Traeth Penllech

Porth Ty-llwyd

GRID REF **SH 188333**
GPS **52.8662°N, 4.6922°W**
COUNTY **Gwynedd**
BEACH FACES **West**

Lithfaen
Pwllheli

Porth Ty-llwyd is a completely rocky cove, backed by grassy slopes and rocks. A rock platform on the south side, high above the sea, is a popular fishing spot.

Porth Colmon

GRID REF **SH 195342**
GPS **52.8746°N, 4.6824°W**
COUNTY **Gwynedd**
BEACH FACES **North-west**

Lithfaen
Pwllheli

Porth Colmon is a small cove of gravelly sand, often used for boat launching. The car park which overlooks the beach is a good spot for watching the waves on a stormy day, and access is down a slipway.

Traeth Penllech

GRID REF **SH 203344**
GPS **52.8766°N, 4.6706°W**
COUNTY **Gwynedd**
BEACH FACES **North-west**

Lithfaen
Pwllheli

Almost a mile long, Traeth Penllech is a beach of sand, rocks and rock pools, backed by boulder clay banks and low cliffs. Signs warn of strong currents, so care needs to be taken if swimming.

The Afon Fawr drops into a small gorge before emerging on to the shore, and a free parking and picnic area can be found at grid ref: SH 206340 (GPS: 52.8746°N, 4.6670°W). From here access to the shore is along a footpath on the opposite side of the Afon Fawr.

Porth Ychain

GRID REF **SH 210360**
GPS **52.8912°N, 4.6611°W**
COUNTY **Gwynedd**
BEACH FACES **North-west**

One of many coves on the north coast of the Llŷn Peninsula, Porth Ychain, which translates as 'Cove of the Oxen', is a beach of shingle and small patches of sand. Access is from the coastal path which runs along the back of the beach. A public footpath runs directly from the nearby lane at grid ref: SH 218360 (GPS: 52.8920°N, 4.6496°W), but parking can be difficult, so it would probably be best to park at Porth Ysgaden and take the coastal path from there.

Porth Gwylan

GRID REF **SH 216368**
GPS **52.8986°N, 4.6526°W**
COUNTY **Gwynedd**
BEACH FACES **North-west**

Porth Gwylan, which translates as 'Seagull Cove', lies approximately half a mile south of Porth Ysgaden and is a sheltered L-shaped bay consisting of rocks with some low-tide sand. Access is down a wide path leading to some concrete steps, and the nearest parking is at Porth Ysgaden.

Porth Ysgaden

GRID REF **SH 219374**
GPS **52.9041°N, 4.6485°W**
COUNTY **Gwynedd**
BEACH FACES **South-west**

Porth Ysgaden is a narrow, sandy inlet backed by cliffs of boulder clay, reached via a long track which leads to a small parking area on the clifftop with extensive sea views. Access to

the shore is then down a steep slipway, only accessible to authorised vehicles. A popular location for scuba diving, this beach is quite sheltered for sunbathing, although there is often an accumulation of sea-borne debris at the back of the beach.

Originally known as Porth Sgaden, the name translates as 'Herring Cove'. On the headland overlooking the cove is the remaining gable end of a cottage, which was once the home of the local customs officer.

Porth y Cychod & Porth Llydan

Porth y Cychod

GRID REF **SH 220375**
GPS **52.9050°N, 4.6471°W**
COUNTY **Gwynedd**
BEACH FACES **North**

Lithfaen
Pwllheli

Just a few minutes' walk from the small, free parking area at Porth Ysgaden, the names of Porth y Cychod and Porth Llydan translate as 'Cove of the Boats' and 'Wide Cove' respectively.

Porth y Cychod is about forty metres wide, and is a cove of shingle, backed by grassy banks which are home to several dilapidated shacks.

Just to the east is Porth Llydan, a similar cove of shingle backed by grassy banks, about 110 metres wide.

Porth Ysglaig & Porth Caseg

Porth Ysglaig

GRID REF **SH 226374**
GPS **52.9043°N, 4.6381°W**
COUNTY **Gwynedd**
BEACH FACES **North-west**

Porth Caseg

GRID REF **SH 228375**
GPS **52.9053°N, 4.6352°W**
COUNTY **Gwynedd**
BEACH FACES **North-west**

Lithfaen
Pwllheli

Approximately 150 metres, Porth Ysglaig is a beach of shingle and a few patches of sand, backed by grass-covered slopes with a caravan park to the eastern side.

To the east is a small headland, the other side of which is Porth Caseg. A tiny cove of coarse sand and rocks backed by grassy slopes, it lies 200 metres west of the much busier Porth Towyn. The nearest parking is at Porth Towyn.

Porth Towyn

GRID REF **SH 231378**
GPS **52.9081°N, 4.6309°W**
COUNTY **Gwynedd**
BEACH FACES **North-west**

Located north-west of the village of Tudweiliog, Porth Towyn is a 200-metre-wide popular sandy bay. When dry, the sand makes a squeaky sound when walked on, similar to the nearby (and better known) Whistling Sands.

Some roadside parking is available on the lane behind the beach, but additional parking, serviced by an honesty box, is usually provided at Towyn Farm. Access to the shore is a walk of about 200 metres down a good path. Facilities include a tearoom and craft shop, and a dog ban operates from April to September inclusive.

Porth Pengallt

GRID REF **SH 232377**
GPS **52.9072°N, 4.6293°W**
COUNTY **Gwynedd**
BEACH FACES **North-west**

Located just north east of Porth Towyn is Porth Pengallt, a sheltered cove which divides into three smaller coves after mid tide, two of which are linked by a small rock arch. Access is a scramble down the grass-covered slopes or by walking around the point from Porth Towyn at low tide.

Porth Bieg & Porth Pant Gwyn

Porth Bieg

GRID REF **SH 236383**
GPS **52.9127°N, 4.6237°W**
COUNTY **Gwynedd**
BEACH FACES **North-west**

Porth Bieg and Porth Pant Gwyn are essentially one long beach of coarse sand, rocks and shingle, with seaweed-covered rocks lower down. Porth Bieg can be reached by taking the coastal path north-east from Porth Towyn for about a third of a mile, where it drops down to near beach level.

Porth Pant Gwyn is about 900 metres north-east of Porth Towyn, reached by taking the coastal path until it crosses the Afon Mynachdy, where waterfalls drop on to the shore. It's possible to scramble down to the shore at this point, but something resembling a path can be found further east.

Traeth Cwmistir

GRID REF **SH 254398**
GPS **52.9268°N, 4.5978°W**
COUNTY **Gwynedd**
BEACH FACES **North**

Traeth Cwmistir is a beach of shingle and a few large rocks on the Llŷn Peninsula's north coast. Backed by banks of boulder clay, access to the shore is down a short permissive path from the coastal path.

Porth Brynogolwyd

GRID REF **SH 257398**
GPS **52.9269°N, 4.5933°W**
COUNTY **Gwynedd**
BEACH FACES **North**

Porth Brynogolwyd is a small cove backed by low cliffs and a waterfall. A cave immediately west of the waterfall was, according to local folklore, a smugglers' tunnel leading to a nearby farm. As with most such tales it's not true, as the cave is only fifteen metres long!

Porth Bryn Gwydd

GRID REF **SH 258399**
GPS **52.9278°N, 4.5919°W**
COUNTY **Gwynedd**
BEACH FACES **North-west**

Porth Bryn Gwydd is a small and little visited shingle cove on the northern coast of the Llŷn Peninsula. Backed by a small valley, access is by public footpath from the nearby lane, Lon Cae Glas, or from the coastal path which drops down to beach level.

Porth Ty-Mawr

GRID REF **SH 261402**
GPS **52.9306°N, 4.5876°W**
COUNTY **Gwynedd**
BEACH FACES **North-west**

Located near the village of Groesffordd, Porth Ty-Mawr is a small cove of sand and shingle backed by steep banks of boulder clay. Parking can be found in the village, and the beach can be reached by a public footpath from the nearby Lon Cae Glas.

233

1 Aber Geirch **2** Borth Wen **3** Porthdinllaen, from above **4** Porthdinllaen

Aber Geirch

GRID REF **SH 264404**
GPS **52.9325°N, 4.5832°W**
COUNTY **Gwynedd**
BEACH FACES **North-west**

Aber Geirch sits at the end of a small and often muddy valley near the village of Edern. The Afon Geirch flows across the beach, which consists mostly of shingle and rotting seaweed. A pipeline runs along the north side. Access is from the coastal path, which crosses the back of the beach.

Borth Wen

GRID REF **SH 273411**
GPS **52.9391°N, 4.5702°W**
COUNTY **Gwynedd**
BEACH FACES **North-west**

Borth Wen is a beach of rocks, shingle and some small patches of sand. It's backed by steep banks of sand and boulder clay, at the top of which is the coastal path and a golf course. Access is by scrambling down the banks.

Porthdinllaen

GRID REF **SH 276415**
GPS **52.9428°N, 4.5660°W**
COUNTY **Gwynedd**
BEACH FACES **North**

the approximate centre point of the bay, and a National Trust car park is located just above it on the clifftop. Beach access is then down a steep path with steps. Dog restrictions apply east of Lon Bridin from 1 April until 30 September. Facilities include toilets and a cafe, and despite this being a good beach for kayaking, sunbathing and swimming, there can be strong currents near the headlands. Conditions can be favourable for surfing, just after high tide being the best time.

A small, secret cove is located near the lifeboat station on the headland, and can be reached via a rocky path along the western side of the bay.

Once considered as the rail terminus and departure point for Ireland, Porthdinllaen is a crescent-shaped sandy beach about one and a quarter miles long, backed by boulder clay cliffs and bounded on the west side by the headland of Trwyn Porth Dinllaen. The popular Ty Coch Inn is at the western end, almost on the beach.

A lane, Lon Bridin, leads on to the shore at

235

1 **Porth Nefyn,** the harbour end at high tide   2 **Porth Bodeilias**   3 **Porth Nefyn**

Porth Nefyn & Porth Bodeilias

Porth Nefyn

GRID REF **SH 300408**
GPS **52.9373°N, 4.5299°W**
COUNTY **Gwynedd**
BEACH FACES **North**

Lithfaen
Pwllheli

Between the headlands of Penrhyn Nefyn and Penrhyn Bodeilias is a mile-and-a-half-long sheltered bay, backed by steep boulder clay banks. The section of the sandy beach below Nefyn village is known as Porth Nefyn, and the extreme eastern end as Porth Bodeilias.

Porth Nefyn is mostly sand with a small harbour and beach huts. Swimming is generally safe, and the high cliffs provide shelter for sunbathing.

Porth Bodeilias is a mix of coarse sand and shingle, backed by steep boulder clay slopes, and this part of the beach is much quieter. Access from Nefyn village is down the steep Lon y Traeth, which leads to a free parking area with space for about twenty vehicles overlooking the shore. Toilets are located halfway down the hill, and dog restrictions apply west of the car park from 1 April to 30 September. A beach warden is in attendance during the summer.

Porth Pistyll

GRID REF **SH 327429**
GPS **52.9570°N, 4.4909°W**
COUNTY **Gwynedd**
BEACH FACES **North-west**

Lithfaen
Pwllheli

Just over a mile long, Porth Pistyll is a little-visited beach situated between the headlands of Penrhyn Bodeilias and Penrhyn Glas. The shore consists of pebbles and low-tide sand, backed by boulder clay banks. At the southern end are the remains of a jetty, once used for loading granite from the quarries.

A small lane off the B4417 north of Pistyll village leads to St Beuno's church. A parking area is just a few metres down this lane, at grid ref: SH 329421 (GPS: 52.9508°N, 4.4875°W), with further lay-by parking on the B4417. To reach the beach, turn right at the church and into a field, heading for a small gate at the opposite corner.

Porth Howel & Porth y Nant

Porth y Nant

GRID REF **SH 344445**
GPS **52.9719°N, 4.4664°W**
COUNTY **Gwynedd**
BEACH FACES **West**

Lithfaen
Pwllheli

Approximately one and a quarter miles long, Porth y Nant is a beach of rocks, pebbles and some low-tide sand situated between the headlands of Trwyn y Gorlech and Penrhyn Glas. Just above the beach is the former quarrying village of Nant Gwrtheyrn, which is now a

centre for the teaching of the Welsh language. Reached via a long, steep lane from Llithfaen, this centre has a car park, visitor centre, shop and a cafe. Final access to the beach is down a steep path.

At Porth y Nant's southern end is the tiny cove of Porth Howel, which has a shore of mostly shingle, backed by steeply sloping banks of scree. Access can be slightly perilous, and you should not attempt to visit this beach unless you are confident you can do so safely. The shortest way to reach Porth Howel is to follow a footpath from the B4417 west of Llithfaen, at grid ref: SH 344429 (GPS: 52.9581°N, 4.4665°W).

West End Beach (Traeth yr Eifl)

GRID REF **SH 362469**
GPS **52.9940°N, 4.4409°W**
COUNTY **Gwynedd**
BEACH FACES **North-west**

Lithfaen
Pwllheli

West End Beach is to the west of the village of Trefor on the Llŷn Peninsula's northern coast. The beach is overlooked by the former granite quarries, and unsurprisingly the larger rocks on the foreshore are mostly granite. The lower shore consists of a variety of smaller pebbles from the boulder clay which backs part of the beach, and some small areas of sand.

The village of Trefor has a small car park opposite the former chapel, at grid ref: SH 371466 (GPS: 52.9925°N, 4.4280°W). From the car park, continue along the lane taking a footpath along a track on the right, passing under a small bridge which carried a tramway to the quarries. Follow this path, bearing right on to the National Trust Nant Bach property and past West End cottages, where the path descending to the shore can be seen.

Trefor

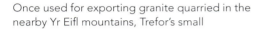

GRID REF **SH 375473**
GPS **52.9980°N, 4.4217°W**
COUNTY **Gwynedd**
BEACH FACES **North**

Once used for exporting granite quarried in the nearby Yr Eifl mountains, Trefor's small

harbour now shelters a small sandy beach about a hundred metres wide, overlooked by two free parking areas. A concrete pier extends beyond the harbour walls, but has been declared unsafe and appears ready to collapse at any time. The immediate shore in both directions is rocky and backed by boulder clay banks.

Facilities include seasonal toilets, picnic tables and a slipway on to the sand. Swimming is generally safe within the harbour area.

Tan y Graig & Gyrn Goch

Tan y Graig

GRID REF **SH 381472**
GPS **52.9973°N, 4.4127°W**
COUNTY **Gwynedd**
BEACH FACES **North-west**

....

Gyrn Goch

GRID REF **SH 395485**
GPS **53.0094°N, 4.3925°W**
COUNTY **Gwynedd**
BEACH FACES **North-west**

Tan y Graig is one of the Llŷn Peninsula's secret and least visited beaches. The half-mile crescent-shaped beach is a mix of sand, shingle and rocks, backed by boulder clay banks which are showing signs of serious erosion.

The old road through Tan y Graig now ends in a cyclepath, and roadside parking can be found here. The footpath from here to the beach has become neglected, and alternative access is a good public footpath through Bryn-yr-Eryr, off a minor road approximately three quarters of a mile to the north-east, at grid ref: SH 393478 (GPS: 53.0030°N, 4.3963°W).

At Gyrn Goch, a campsite overlooks a beach of shingle and patches of sand, backed by low cliffs of sand and boulder clay. The Afon Hen issues on to the shore and access from the site is down a slipway. Note that there is no public right of way through the campsite, and the closest alternative access is the footpath through Bryn-yr-Eryr, about half a mile to the south-west.

Clynnog Fawr

GRID REF **SH 408499**
GPS **53.0223°N, 4.3739°W**
COUNTY **Gwynedd**
BEACH FACES **West**

The small village of Clynnog Fawr has a beach of rocks, shingle and some low-tide sand, backed by low cliffs of boulder clay.

Roadside parking can be found in the village, and from here a footpath on the south-west side of St Beuno's church leads across the A499, continuing in a straight line for a quarter of a mile to the beach. Final access to the shore is down a short flight of steps. A short distance back along this path, a track off to the south leads to the ancient burial chamber of Bachwen Dolmen.

Aberdesach

GRID REF **SH 423514**
GPS **53.0362°N, 4.3522°W**
COUNTY **Gwynedd**
BEACH FACES **North-west**

A short lane with some sharp corners leads from the A499 to a free car park overlooking the beach at Aberdesach. The upper shore is a mix of large pebbles, smaller shingle and some sandy patches, backed by banks of boulder clay. Lower down you will find seaweed-covered rocks and some low-tide sand. There are toilets here but no other facilities, and overnight parking is not allowed.

Pontllyfni

GRID REF **SH 429526**
GPS **53.0472°N, 4.3439°W**
COUNTY **Gwynedd**
BEACH FACES **North-west**

Pontllyfni is a beach of rocks, shingle and some coarse sand, backed by low banks of boulder clay. Behind the beach is a grassed area with seating, and a slipway on to the shore. Parking can be found on the east side of the A499 near the river bridge. From here a footpath leads alongside the river to a rocky shore, but the better part of the beach can be found at the end of a lane 350 metres to the south-west.

1 Dinas Dinlle, shore to the south **2** Dinas Dinlle, from the hill fort
3 Morfa Dinlle, looking south **4** Morfa Dinlle, looking towards Anglesey

Dinas Dinlle & Morfa Dinlle

Dinas Dinlle

GRID REF **SH 435565**
GPS **53.0824°N, 4.3368°W**
COUNTY **Gwynedd**
BEACH FACES **West**

🅿 ☕ 🍴 ⓦⓒ

Morfa Dinlle

GRID REF **SH 432583**
GPS **53.0985°N, 4.3422°W**
COUNTY **Gwynedd**
BEACH FACES **West**

🅿

Llangefni
Bangor
Caernarfon
Lithfaen
Pwllheli

The village of Dinas Dinlle has a beach of coarse sand and shingle, backed by a concrete walkway. The shoreline in both directions is very similar. Free car parking areas are just behind the beach, and access to the shore is up easy ramps or steps to the walkway, which is level with the shingle at the back of the beach.

This is a very exposed beach with no shelter from the wind, and swimming is not advisable due to fast currents. A dog ban operates between the two groynes on the beach (approximately 275 metres) from 1 April until 30 September, and facilities include toilets, drinking water, cold water showers, cafes, beach shops and a children's play area. The skyline to the south is dominated by the Yr Eifl mountains.

Morfa Dinlle is about a mile further north, and has a low-tide sandy beach backed by a high storm bank of pebbles. Parking areas on rough ground are located between the road and the shore almost all the way between the two.

The island of Anglesey lies across the Menai Strait from mainland Wales, and though it is not particularly hilly it's rarely flat. Superbly picturesque, the countryside is dotted with small outcrops of rock which are clad with vibrant yellow gorse flowers in spring.

Holyhead is the largest town, containing a mainline railway station and ferry terminal. Nearby, Holyhead Mountain is the island's highest point at 220 metres. There's little heavy traffic, and the well-maintained roads and footpaths prove a good choice for cycling, walking, wildlife and photography.

The main beaches are to the south-east, while the north-western half of the island has numerous tiny coves. It is easy to have one of these to yourself, even at the height of summer. During the summer beach wardens attend the main beaches, but there are no lifeguards.

ANGLESEY

Opposite Traeth Abermenai

Tal-y-Foel Beach

GRID REF **SH 478650**
GPS **53.1600°N, 4.2767°W**
COUNTY **Isle of Anglesey**
BEACH FACES **South-east**

Situated on the Anglesey side of the Menai Strait, Tal-y-Foel beach isn't a place for paddling and sandcastles. There can be strong currents and swimming can be dangerous. The shore consists of shingle, seaweed and some small patches of coarse sand. A parking area for about six cars on a lane connecting to the B4419 overlooks the Strait, with good views towards Caernarvon and the mountains of Snowdonia.

Traeth Abermenai

GRID REF **SH 436629**
GPS **53.1399°N, 4.3385°W**
COUNTY **Isle of Anglesey**
BEACH FACES **East**

Traeth Abermenai (also known as Traeth Melynog) is a wide, featureless bay of wet sand, fringed with glasswort and bordered by a narrow band of salt marsh (see page 247). At the extreme south-eastern end near Abermenai Point the salt marsh gives way to a sheltered shore backed by dunes, over which the eastern end of Newborough Beach is 100 metres away.

A small free parking area has space for about six cars, and is located at grid ref: SH 432643 (GPS: 53.1538°N, 4.3461°W). To get here, take the south exit at the Pen-lon roundabout on the A4080. From the car park, a straight footpath of just under a mile crosses Newborough Warren to the shore – beware of horse flies here in the summer. Abermenai Point is then a similar distance across the sands. If crossing the sands on foot be aware that the sand will flood quickly on an incoming tide.

Newborough Beach (Traeth Llanddwyn)

GRID REF **SH 405633**
GPS **53.1426°N, 4.3850°W**
COUNTY **Isle of Anglesey**
BEACH FACES **South**

Newborough Beach (correctly known as Traeth Llanddwyn) is a three-and-a-half-mile sandy beach reaching from Llanddwyn Island to Abermenai Point. The fine sand on the shore also has small amounts of shingle, backed by dunes. Further back are Newborough Forest and the Nature Reserve of Newborough Warren. There are plenty of things to look out for in the forest; red squirrels can often be seen, and flora to be found in the warren include marsh and dune helleborines, butterwort and round-leaved wintergreen. The forest also has various waymarked trails, including a 6.8-mile route for runners.

A car park is situated in the forest behind the beach, and is reached by turning off the A4080 in Newborough village along Llys Rhosyr, which leads to a toll road. Beach access is a short walk over the dunes. Facilities include toilets, cold water showers, picnic tables, barbecue areas, cycle stands, drinking water and usually refreshment vans in summer. Swimming is generally safe on most of the beach, but there are currents towards Abermenai Point. Dog restrictions apply west of the main access point as far as Llanddwyn Island, from 1 April to 30 September.

Llanddwyn Island

Porth y Cwch

GRID REF **SH 391631**
GPS **53.1404°N, 4.4058°W**
COUNTY **Isle of Anglesey**
BEACH FACES **East**

Beach	Grid Ref	Translation
Porth y Cwch	SH391631	Boat Cove
Porth yr Halen	SH391629	Salt Cove
Porth y Clochydd	SH388627	Sexton Cove
Pilot's Cove	SH386624	–
Porth Twr Bach	SH386623	Small Tower Cove
Porth Twr Mawr	SH385624	Big Tower Cove
Porth yr Ogof	SH386629	Cove of the Cave

Llanddwyn Island is about three quarters of a mile long and only becomes cut off at high tide, but is usually just a short paddle across from Newborough Beach. The whitewashed lighthouse on the island is a prominent feature of the southern Anglesey coast, and the island's beaches are small sandy coves. The table left lists them in a clockwise direction, beginning at the crossing point.

The name 'Llanddwyn' translates as 'Church of St Dwynwen', St Dwynwen being the Welsh patron saint of lovers, who is commemorated annually on 25 January. The evocative remains of the church can be seen towards the south-west of the island. There's plenty to explore and some unusual flora to be found, including henbane, marsh orchids, yellow horned poppies, bloody cranesbill and dune pansies. Pebbles to be found on the shores include pillow lavas, green schist and jasper. The nearest parking is at Newborough Beach, and dogs are not allowed from 1 May to 30 September.

Malltraeth Bay

GRID REF **SH 389639**
GPS **53.1500°N, 4.4102°W**
COUNTY **Isle of Anglesey**
BEACH FACES **South-west**

Malltraeth Bay is ideal for those seeking a beautiful sandy beach without the crowds. Situated between Llanddwyn Island and the Cefni estuary, it's a mile and a half long and about a mile's walk from the nearest car park at Newborough Forest. The beach is backed by a line of tall dunes, with Newborough Forest further back. Green pillow lavas outcrop at the southern end near Llanddwyn Island. At the approximate midpoint of the beach are the remains of the *Athena*, a Greek ship wrecked in 1852.

Dogs are allowed, but as restrictions apply on the western end of Newborough Beach from 1 April to 30 September, they would need to be walked through the forest. Alternative access to the remote northern end would be from a small car park in Newborough Forest just off the A4080, at grid ref: SH 411670 (GPS: 53.1768°N, 4.3792°W), but it's over an hour's walk from here.

Bodorgan

Porth Cadwaladr

GRID REF **SH 361665**
GPS **53.1700°N, 4.4523°W**
COUNTY **Isle of Anglesey**
BEACH FACES **South-west**

The private estate of Bodorgan (emphasis on the second syllable) on the southern coast of Anglesey is bounded to the south by the Afon Cefni estuary and to the north by the dune system of Tywyn Aberffraw. There is **no public access** to this however, as the Anglesey coastal path takes an inland diversion around it.

The shoreline consists of a series of small, intimate sandy coves flanked by low cliffs and backed by dunes. As they are **inaccessible to the public**, these coves have been protected against commercialisation and caravan parks, remaining much as they have been for hundreds of years. The beaches in clockwise direction are Porth y Ddraenen-wen (SH 372651), Porth Cerig-cochion (SH 370650), Porth Fain (SH 368651), Porth Gro (SH 367652), Porth Buarth-y-mor (SH 367654), Porth Tywyn-mawr (SH 366656), Porth y Cwch (SH 363658), Porth Cae-ceffylau (SH 362662) and Porth Cadwaladr (SH 361665).

Aberffraw Bay (Traeth Mawr)

GRID REF **SH 354676**
GPS **53.1797°N, 4.4634°W**
COUNTY **Isle of Anglesey**
BEACH FACES **South-west**

Aberffraw Bay (pronounced 'Abber-frown' without the final 'n') is a half-mile-wide sandy beach backed by the extensive dune system of Tywyn Aberffraw. A free car parking area is located just off the A4080 east of Aberffraw village, and access to the beach is a walk of approximately 900 metres along the sandy Afon Ffraw estuary. The beach has no facilities, but Aberffraw village has a cafe, seasonal toilets, a pub and a small shop. Aberffraw is one of Anglesey's surf beaches, with the best breaks usually occurring by the river mouth. However, dangerous rips occur here so it's not one for beginners.

Porth Lleidiog

GRID REF **SH 349677**
GPS **53.1814°N, 4.4709°W**
COUNTY **Isle of Anglesey**
BEACH FACES **South**

Porth Lleidiog is a beach of coarse sand, backed by banks of boulder clay, rocks and rock pools at low tide. The nearest parking is just off the A4080 at Aberffraw and access is via the coastal path along the west side of the Afon Ffraw. The beach itself has no facilities, but it's a good spot for shell collecting and escaping the crowds, and the nearby Aberffraw village has a pub, a small shop and toilets.

Porth Terfyn

GRID REF **SH 343676**
GPS **53.1805°N, 4.4807°W**
COUNTY **Isle of Anglesey**
BEACH FACES **South-west**

Located on the east side of the Braich-lwyd headland, Porth Terfyn is a small beach of shingle and some sand, with a tiny, sandy cove to one side. Reaching the shore involves a short scramble down the rocks on the east side. Its name translates as 'Boundary Cove'.

Porth Aels

GRID REF **SH 338673**
GPS **53.1765°N, 4.4871°W**
COUNTY **Isle of Anglesey**
BEACH FACES **South-west**

Porth Aels is a beach of coarse sand and rock pools west of the Braich-lwyd headland. Access is down a short path to the east side. Although this beach is sheltered and good for sunbathing, there can be noise from the nearby motor-racing circuit.

Porth Cwyfan & Porth China

GRID REF **SH 338681**
GPS **53.1837°N, 4.4875°W**
COUNTY **Isle of Anglesey**
BEACH FACES **South-west**

The twelfth-century Church of St Cwyfan once stood on a peninsula separating the coves of Porth Cwyfan and Porth China. Over the years, the soft boulder clay has been eroded, and now it's effectively one large beach, with the church stranded on a walled island in the centre of the bay. Services are still held there in the summer.

The upper shore is coarse sand and shingle, backed by low banks of boulder clay, with agricultural land behind. Lower down it's mostly seaweed-covered rocks. Some roadside parking is available at the end of Stryd yr Eglwys from Aberffraw village – but the surface and width of this lane are deteriorating on the approach to the beach.

Porth Trecastell (Cable Bay)

GRID REF **SH 333707**
GPS **53.2069°N, 4.4964°W**
COUNTY **Isle of Anglesey**
BEACH FACES **West**

Porth Trecastell, or Cable Bay, is a sheltered sandy bay backed by dunes and edged by rock pools and cliffs. This is a good beach for swimming and sunbathing. A small parking area is situated just off the A4080, from where access to the beach is a short walk over the dunes. Opposite the parking area, a footpath can be followed to Ty Croes Railway Station, which is roughly a mile and a half away.

On the headland to the north is the burial chamber of Barclodiad y Gawres, internal viewings of which can be arranged – check local notices for further information.

Porth Nobla & Porth Tyn Tywyn

GRID REF **SH 328714**
GPS **53.2130°N, 4.5042°W**
COUNTY **Isle of Anglesey**
BEACH FACES **West**

Porth Nobla and Porth Tyn Tywyn are two adjoining beaches of coarse sand and shingle. At high tide the rocks in the bay become small islets, one of which has its own tiny beach. Parking is at a small car park situated just off the A4080, from where access to the shore is a walk of about fifty metres across the low dunes.

Traeth Llydan (Broad Beach)

GRID REF **SH 319724**
GPS **53.2217°N, 4.5182°W**
COUNTY **Isle of Anglesey**
BEACH FACES **South-west**

Rhosneigr's eastern beach is known as Traeth Llydan – a wide beach of coarse sand backed by dunes. East of the village, the A4080 has a wide gravelled verge along its northern side for parking and from here public footpaths lead across the dunes to the beach. Alternative parking can be found at Rhosneigr.

1 Rhosneigr Beach   **2** Traeth Crigyll   **3** Traeth Cymyran

Rhosneigr Beach

GRID REF **SH 316730**
GPS **53.2270°N, 4.5230°W**
COUNTY **Isle of Anglesey**
BEACH FACES **West**

Rhosneigr's sandy beach lies west of the village, and is a popular location for watersports. Swimming is generally safe but rip currents can occur, and to the south are some rocky islets.

Access from the village is down roads which lead on to the shore. Parking can be found at the library and at the northern end of the village. Local facilities include cafes, toilets, a beach shop and pubs. Rhosneigr Railway Station is about three quarters of a mile away.

Traeth Crigyll

GRID REF **SH 314736**
GPS **53.2323°N, 4.5263°W**
COUNTY **Isle of Anglesey**
BEACH FACES **South-west**

Traeth Crigyll is a sandy beach to the north-west of Rhosneigr, backed by dunes and the RAF Valley airfield. The Afon Crigyll emerges on to the shore, which is contiguous with Traeth Cymyran, forming essentially one long beach with the rocky islet of Ynys Feirig acting as the dividing line.

The nearest parking is at Rhosneigr. Conditions for surfing are best around mid tide dropping off towards the high, but rocks can be a hazard.

Traeth Cymyran

GRID REF **SH 300750**
GPS **53.2444°N, 4.5480°W**
COUNTY **Isle of Anglesey**
BEACH FACES **South-west**

Unsurprisingly there is considerable aircraft activity, so it is not a place for peace and quiet.

A small parking area is located behind the dunes at grid ref: SH 297755 (GPS: 53.2500°N, 4.5522°W), and can be reached by taking Cymyran Road from the A5 in Caergeiliog. Alternative access is along Traeth Crigyll from Rhosneigr.

Swimming is dangerous at the western end due to currents.

Traeth Cymyran is a sandy beach backed by dunes and the RAF Valley airfield.

Silver Bay

GRID REF **SH 289752**
GPS **53.2459°N, 4.5646°W**
COUNTY **Isle of Anglesey**
BEACH FACES **South**

Originally known as Traeth Llydan, this beach is now commonly known as Silver Bay, after the holiday village which adjoins its western end. The crescent-shaped sandy bay, which is 550 metres wide, has a few high-tide rocky islets, and is backed by dunes and a small coniferous plantation. It looks out across Cymyran Bay towards Rhosneigr. A colourful variety of pebbles can be found, including quartz, jasper and various sandstones.

This is a popular beach for kayaking and occasionally surfing, but there can be frequent noise from the aircrafts at the nearby RAF Valley airfield. There is no public car park (or space to park) anywhere near – the best places to park are Rhoscolyn or Borthwen – and all public access is via the coastal path.

Porth yr Ych & Porth Gorslwyn

GRID REF **SH 287750**
GPS **53.2440°N, 4.5675°W**
COUNTY **Isle of Anglesey**
BEACH FACES **South-east**

These small, sheltered coves lie just west of Silver Bay on Anglesey's Holy Island, and are backed by low cliffs and the coastal path.

The upper shores consist of light shingle and small patches of sand, with rocks, seaweed and rock pools lower down.

Porth yr Ych is the first beach west of Silver Bay and access involves a fairly easy climb down the rocks on either side. Porth Gorslwyn is a little further west, and access is from the coastal path which drops down to beach level. Their names translate as 'Ox Cove' and 'Marshgrove Cove' respectively.

Porth Cae-du

GRID REF **SH 280748**
GPS **53.2420°N, 4.5779°W**
COUNTY **Isle of Anglesey**
BEACH FACES **South**

Porth Cae-du is a narrow cove of sand and rocks on the south side of Holy Island, just a short walk from Borthwen. Its name translates as 'Black Field Cove'.

Borthwen

GRID REF **SH 272750**
GPS **53.2446°N, 4.5907°W**
COUNTY **Isle of Anglesey**
BEACH FACES **South**

Borthwen, also known as Rhoscolyn Beach, is a sandy bay backed by low dunes, with some smaller coves to either side. The beach's pay & display car park is small and can be reached along a lane from Rhoscolyn, which is extremely narrow with sharp corners, and barely enough space for cars and pedestrians to pass. If the car park is full vehicles must return to the village, where some roadside parking is available. To avoid walking along the narrow lane if parking in the village, take a public footpath on the left at the rear of the church.

Beach facilities include seasonal toilets and cold water showers. Access to the shore is a slipway or a short, sandy path. A beach warden is on duty from the end of May until early September.

Porth y Corwgl

GRID REF **SH 270747**
GPS **53.2412°N, 4.5928°W**
COUNTY **Isle of Anglesey**
BEACH FACES **South**

Porth y Corwgl (one of three Anglesey beaches with this name) lies just to the south-west of Borthwen Beach, and is generally much quieter than its neighbour. It looks out towards the islands of Ynysoedd Gwylanod.

Porth Saint

GRID REF **SH 259759**
GPS **53.2512°N, 4.6099°W**
COUNTY **Isle of Anglesey**
BEACH FACES **South**

Although the rocky cove of Porth Saint does not have any sand, it does have some geological interest due to the pink-coloured rocks of Holyhead quartzite, and the orange rocks of sandstone stained with iron oxide.

The cove is named after St Gwenfaen, a female saint who, according to legend, in the sixth century escaped from druids by climbing a sea stack in this bay.

Access is down a gully from the coastal path, with a short scramble at the bottom.

Porth-y-garan

GRID REF **SH 256771**
GPS **53.2619°N, 4.6151°W**
COUNTY **Isle of Anglesey**
BEACH FACES **West**

Porth-y-garan is a small inlet on Anglesey's Holy Island which divides into smaller coves on the high tide. The shore is shingle with some small patches of sand, and is backed by a caravan park.

The nearest roadside parking is towards the end of Ravenspoint Road, but suitable places are quickly taken. Alternative parking would be as for Trearddur Bay.

Porth Castell & Porth Diana

Porth Castell

GRID REF **SH 252781**
GPS **53.2707°N, 4.6216°W**
COUNTY **Isle of Anglesey**
BEACH FACES **West**

Porth Diana

GRID REF **SH 254783**
GPS **53.2726°N, 4.6187°W**
COUNTY **Isle of Anglesey**
BEACH FACES **West**

Porth Castell and Porth Diana are two neighbouring sandy coves, just a short walk south of Trearddur Bay on Anglesey's Holy Island. Both are backed by a sea wall and flanked by rocks of mica schist.

Porth Diana is the larger of the two, and is often used by the local yacht club for moorings. Porth Castell is just to the south, and is a better choice for swimming. Ravenspoint Road runs behind the beaches and roadside parking is possible further along the lane, but suitable places are readily taken. Alternative parking is at Trearddur Bay.

Behind Porth Diana, a public footpath off Ravenspoint Road leads to the Porth Diana Nature Reserve, where Anglesey's county flower – the spotted rock-rose – can be seen during early summer.

Trearddur Bay

GRID REF **SH 255788**
GPS **53.2771°N, 4.6175°W**
COUNTY **Isle of Anglesey**
BEACH FACES **South-west**

Amlwch

Valley

Llangefni

Trearddur Bay (pronounced 'Tree-are-the') lies roughly two miles south of Holyhead on Anglesey's Holy Island. Its sandy beach is backed by a sea wall, promenade and plenty of seating, and access is down steps or a slipway. Some smaller sandy coves lie to either side of the main beach, and rocks in the centre of the bay become tiny islets at high tide.

Facilities include restaurants, seasonal toilets, drinking water, refreshment vans (in summer), cycle parking and a shop. Two pay & display car parks, with a height restriction of 1.9 metres, are nearby, and some short-term roadside parking is also available.

A dog ban operates on the southern half of the beach from May to September inclusive, and beach wardens are on duty during the summer. Surf conditions can be good around mid tide, particularly if other beaches are blown out, but the rocks can be a hazard.

Porth Isallt Bach & Porth yr Afon

Porth yr Afon

GRID REF **SH 248792**
GPS **53.2811°N, 4.6282°W**
COUNTY **Isle of Anglesey**
BEACH FACES **South-west**

Porth Isallt Bach and Porth yr Afon are the first of a series of small sheltered coves alongside Lon Isallt, north of Trearddur Bay. The shore is a mix of shingle and sand, and the surrounding rocks are of mica schist. Parking near these beaches is difficult, but Trearddur Bay with its facilities is just a short walk away.

Porth y Pwll

GRID REF **SH 243793**
GPS **53.2818°N, 4.6356°W**
COUNTY **Isle of Anglesey**
BEACH FACES **South-west**

Porth y Pwll is the third of a series of small sheltered coves north of Trearddur Bay, consisting of sand and shingle, backed by a sea wall and a road (Lon Isallt). Some parking is possible behind it on the verge, otherwise parking is at Trearddur Bay.

Porth-y-Post

GRID REF **SH 242794**
GPS **53.2820°N, 4.6373°W**
COUNTY **Isle of Anglesey**
BEACH FACES **West**

Porth-y-Post is one of a series of small, sheltered sandy coves along the west coast of Holy Island. Approximately ninety metres wide, it's backed by a sea wall and flanked by rocks and low cliffs of mica schist. The sea is often crystal clear in summer and ideal for swimming. Some roadside parking is available behind the beach and access to the shore is down a few steps.

Porth y Corwgl

GRID REF **SH 240796**
GPS **53.2848°N, 4.6407°W**
COUNTY **Isle of Anglesey**
BEACH FACES **West**

Just north of Porth-y-Post, Porth y Corwgl (one of three Anglesey beaches with this name) is a small cove of sand and shingle about fifty metres wide, backed by low cliffs. Access is by public footpath from Lon Isallt.

Porth Dafarch

GRID REF **SH 233799**
GPS **53.2862°N, 4.6511°W**
COUNTY **Isle of Anglesey**
BEACH FACES **South-west**

shore is down steps or a slipway.

Although this is a popular beach for swimming, canoeing, surfing, coasteering and scuba diving, launching of powered crafts is not allowed. Facilities include toilets, drinking water, cycle stands, picnic tables and refreshment vans in summer. Holyhead Railway Station is approximately one and three quarters of a mile away, and the beach can be reached along the appropriately named Porthdafarch Road – a mostly rural road with a pavement all the way. A dog ban operates from 1 May until 30 September, and a beach warden is on duty during the summer.

Owned by the National Trust, the sandy cove of Porth Dafarch is one of Anglesey's more popular beaches, lying just over a mile south-west of Holyhead on Holy Island. The shore is backed by a sea wall and a beach access road, where some parking is available. Access to the

Porth Rhwydau

GRID REF **SH 228798**
GPS **53.2857°N, 4.6598°W**
COUNTY **Isle of Anglesey**
BEACH FACES **South-east**

Porth Rhwydau, which translates as 'Cove of the Fishing Nets'. Between mid and high tide it's mostly underwater, but around the low-tide period it's a beach of sand and caves, one of which is twenty metres long.

The nearest parking is at Porth Dafarch, and access from the coastal path is by scrambling down the rocks at the eastern side – an easy descent provided a little time is taken to establish the best route.

A short walk along the coastal path north from Porth Dafarch leads to the sheltered cove of

Porth Ruffydd

GRID REF **SH 224795**
GPS **53.2846°N, 4.6758°W**
COUNTY **Isle of Anglesey**
BEACH FACES **South**

Porth Ruffydd is a narrow, sheltered cove of shingle and some low-tide sand on the west side of Anglesey's Holy Island. A free car parking area can be found at grid ref: SH 216802 (GPS: 53.2901°N, 4.6772°W), and from here a heather-bordered path leads for a quarter of a mile to the coastal path. Final access to the shore is down some concrete steps. This is a good spot for swimming and coasteering, but be wary of strong currents just offshore.

Henborth

GRID REF **SH 214814**
GPS **53.2991°N, 4.6804°W**
COUNTY **Isle of Anglesey**
BEACH FACES **West**

Henborth is a beach of two small coves on the north-west corner of Anglesey's Holy Island. Roadside parking is available at the junction of the lane to South Stack, at grid ref: SH 217815 (GPS: 53.3007°N, 4.6774°W). A narrow path leads to some steep steps which descend to the more southerly, and more rocky, of the two coves. The northern cove is better, consisting of light shingle and small patches of sand backed by high cliffs. A path up the cliffs here is private, and doesn't lead back to the road.

Newry Beach

GRID REF **SH 245833**
GPS **53.3172°N, 4.6350°W**
COUNTY **Isle of Anglesey**
BEACH FACES **North**

Newry is a long, narrow beach of mica schist rocks and shingle, protected by the breakwaters of Holyhead Harbour. The road which runs behind it, appropriately named Beach Road, has plenty of bays for parking. Slipways provide access to the shore, and facilities include toilets and a cafe at the western end.

1 Pwll y Gwman **2** Pwll y Gwman, the way to the shore **3** Penrhos Beach
4 Private Beach **5** Private Beach, looking out across the bay

Pwll y Gwman

GRID REF **SH 259823**
GPS **53.3087°N, 4.6134°W**
COUNTY **Isle of Anglesey**
BEACH FACES **North**

To the east of Holyhead Harbour is Pwll y Gwman; a small beach of shingle, shells and patches of coarse sand, backed by low cliffs. Its name translates as 'Pool of Seaweed'. The tiny islet of Ynys Peibio can be seen in the photo. Backed by playing fields, access is a public footpath across the fields leading to a stone archway. Parking can easily be found in a nearby housing estate.

Penrhos Beach

GRID REF **SH 264817**
GPS **53.3034°N, 4.6056°W**
COUNTY **Isle of Anglesey**
BEACH FACES **North**

Penrhos Beach lies east of Holyhead alongside the A5. The main beach is comprised of sand backed by a grassed area and the coastal path, with low cliffs to the eastern side. Swimming is generally safe. Two small, free parking areas, both with a height restriction of 1.9 metres, are located at either end of the beach just off the A5.

Private Beach

GRID REF **SH 275815**
GPS **53.3020°N, 4.5890°W**
COUNTY **Isle of Anglesey**
BEACH FACES **North-east**

Once part of a private estate and inaccessible (hence the name), Private Beach is a bay of white sand in the Penrhos Coastal Park east of Holyhead. Car parking and toilets for the Coastal Park are found at grid ref: SH 275806 (GPS: 53.2936°N, 4.5895°W) – the first turning on the right from the A5 west of the Stanley Embankment. Access to the beach is then a mostly level walk of about half a mile along good paths.

Gorad Beach

GRID REF **SH 293806**
GPS **53.2945°N, 4.5615°W**
COUNTY **Isle of Anglesey**
BEACH FACES **West**

Lying at the end of Gorad Road, this is very much a 'locals' beach. Backed by boulder clay banks, the upper shore is mostly sand, with a lower shore of seaweed-strewn sand and rocks. The Newlands Park housing estate backs the southern end and parking can easily be found here, and the Afon Alaw emerges to the north.

Porth Penial Dowyn

GRID REF **SH 291829**
GPS **53.3151°N, 4.5658°W**
COUNTY **Isle of Anglesey**
BEACH FACES **West**

Porth Penial Dowyn is a long and little-visited beach of coarse sand and light shingle, backed by agricultural land. It can be reached either along a singletrack lane from the village of Llanfwrog, or by public footpath from Llanfachraeth. Parking near the beach is difficult, but easier to find at either of the two villages.

Porth Penrhyn Mawr

GRID REF **SH 287837**
GPS **53.3221°N, 4.5722°W**
COUNTY **Isle of Anglesey**
BEACH FACES **South-west**

Porth Penrhyn Mawr is a rather untidy beach of sand and shingle with some rocks, backed by banks of boulder clay, and a lower shore of seaweed-strewn rocks. Approximately 450 metres wide, it looks out towards Holyhead, and the road from Llanfwrog to Penrhyn Bay Caravan Park passes its northern end. Access to the shore is down a short track.

Porth Dryw & Porth Delysg

GRID REF **SH 282839**
GPS **53.3238°N, 4.5798°W**
COUNTY **Isle of Anglesey**
BEACH FACES **West**

The Anglesey Coast Path cuts across the neck of the headland of Penrhyn, bypassing these two beaches, but Coast Path walkers aren't missing much. Backed by farmland, both beaches have an upper shore of coarse grey sand and shingle, and a lower shore of seaweed-strewn rocks and sand.

Porth Delysg is 350 metres wide and bounded on the northern side by the Penrhyn Bay Holiday Park, a path from here leading on to the shore. Porth Dryw is 200 metres wide and access is along the shore from either end. A small stream emerges on to the beach via a culvert.

Porth Tywyn Mawr

GRID REF **SH 287851**
GPS **53.3347°N, 4.5729°W**
COUNTY **Isle of Anglesey**
BEACH FACES **West**

Known locally as Sandy Beach, Porth Tywyn Mawr is a half-mile-wide sandy bay, near the village of Llanfwrog. The shore is backed by low dunes and there are several rocky islets in the bay.

Penrhyn Bay Caravan Park occupies the southern headland of this beach, which is very popular for watersports. Limited roadside parking is available at the end of the lane from Llanfwrog at grid ref: SH 289850 (GPS: 53.3342°N, 4.57081°W), and from here access to the shore is down a short track.

Porth Trefadog

GRID REF **SH 290861**
GPS **53.3438°N, 4.5690°W**
COUNTY **Isle of Anglesey**
BEACH FACES **West**

Porth Trefadog is a quiet beach on Anglesey's west coast, reached along narrow lanes from the village of Llanfaethlu. Approximately 275 metres wide, the shore consists of coarse sand and shingle, backed by a low sea wall and a few cottages. A small parking area overlooks the shore.

Porth y Ffynnon

GRID REF **SH 291873**
GPS **53.3546°N, 4.5681°W**
COUNTY **Isle of Anglesey**
BEACH FACES **North-west**

The wide cove of Porth y Ffynnon, which translates as 'Cove of the Spring', lies south of Porth Trwyn, and is a rocky beach with some sand. Backed by low cliffs which drop almost to beach level at the southern end, these provide easy access to the shore.

Porth Fudr

GRID REF **SH 292873**
GPS **53.3546°N, 4.5666°W**
COUNTY **Isle of Anglesey**
BEACH FACES **West**

Just south of Porth Trwyn is a tiny cove with the unfortunate name of Porth Fudr, or 'Dirty Cove', named after the tiny stream of Gwter Fudr ('Dirty Gutter') which empties into it.

Porth Trwyn

GRID REF **SH 295878**
GPS **53.3592°N, 4.5624°W**
COUNTY **Isle of Anglesey**
BEACH FACES **West**

Porth Trwyn is a small beach on Anglesey's west coast, consisting of low-tide sand and rocks with plenty of shingle at the top of the beach. A small, free car park on stony ground is situated between the road and the beach, and access to the shore is along a short track.

Porth Penrhyn

GRID REF **SH 297884**
GPS **53.3647°N, 4.5597°W**
COUNTY **Isle of Anglesey**
BEACH FACES **West**

Porth Penrhyn is a long and little-visited beach of sand and shingle on Anglesey's north-west coast. The easiest way on to the shore is a steep path down a gully at the northern end.

Porth Crugmor

GRID REF **SH 299886**
GPS **53.3665°N, 4.5568°W**
COUNTY **Isle of Anglesey**
BEACH FACES **West**

Porth Crugmor, also known as Cable Bay, is a small, picturesque cove about half a mile south of the more popular Church Bay. The shore consists of shingle, rock pools and low-tide sand. The cliffs to the north have some impressive caves, two of which are connected by an opening big enough to scramble through. Access is from the coastal path which drops down to beach level.

Porth Tyddyn Uchaf

GRID REF **SH 299888**
GPS **53.3683°N, 4.5569°W**
COUNTY **Isle of Anglesey**
BEACH FACES **West**

Located between Porth Crugmor and the tiny shingle cove of Porth y Pren – which is accessible by a steep path – Porth Tyddyn Uchaf is a wide bay of shingle, patches of coarse sand and low-tide rock pools. Access is along the shore from either of its neighbours. The wreck of a vessel, the *Annie*, can be seen at low tide.

Porth y Santes

GRID REF **SH 299890**
GPS **53.3701°N, 4.5570°W**
COUNTY **Isle of Anglesey**
BEACH FACES **West**

Porth y Santes lies just south of Anglesey's Church Bay, and is a small, sheltered cove of sand and shingle. Access is down a short, steep path from the coastal path. The cove between this and Church Bay is Porth y Cychod, and is a beach of rocks and shingle but no sand.

Church Bay (Porth Swtan)

GRID REF **SH 299894**
GPS **53.3737°N, 4.5573°W**
COUNTY **Isle of Anglesey**
BEACH FACES **West**

Church Bay, or Porth Swtan, is one of Anglesey's more popular beaches, and is signposted from the A5025 at Llanrhyddlad. The shore is sandy with rocks, and backed by cliffs of yellow volcanic tuff. Pebbles found on the shore include red jasper, purple and red sandstones, black siltstones and white quartz. The name 'Porth Swtan' translates as 'Whiting Cove'.

Access is down a steep concrete slipway. A beach warden is in attendance during the summer. Facilities include a car park, roadside parking, seasonal toilets, cycle stands and a restaurant. Swimming is also generally safe.

Porth Gwter Fudr

GRID REF **SH 295903**
GPS **53.3817°N, 4.5637°W**
COUNTY **Isle of Anglesey**
BEACH FACES **West**

Porth Gwter Fudr, or 'Dirty Gutter Cove', is a small beach of shingle and rocks. It lies half a mile north of Church Bay and there is no obvious path down. Although it's possible to scramble down the rocks, there can be nesting birds here, so it is best left unvisited.

1 Porth y Bribys   **2** Porth y Nant, from the north   **3** Porth y Nant

Porth y Bribys & Porth y Nant

Porth y Nant

GRID REF **SH 294912**
GPS **53.3897°N, 4.5657°W**
COUNTY **Isle of Anglesey**
BEACH FACES **West**

Amlwch

Valley

Llangefni

About sixty metres wide, Porth y Nant is a very secluded and remote cove of rocks, shingle and some sand, which can be reached by a short but easy scramble down the south side. A small parking area is located at grid ref: SH 303914

(GPS: 53.3926°N, 4.5544°W), and from here a public footpath leads across sheep pastures to the coastal path. Following this south will lead to Porth y Nant, a total distance of three quarters of a mile.

Neighbouring it on the south side is Porth y Bribys. This is a narrow cove of shingle, rocks, rock pools and a small cave. It can be reached by scrambling with great care down a very steep bank and scree slope at the back of the beach. However, there are some burrows here that indicate the presence of nesting birds, so this one is probably best left to nature. The photos show the beaches at mid tide.

Traeth y Fydlyn

GRID REF **SH 290916**
GPS **53.3932°N, 4.5720°W**
COUNTY **Isle of Anglesey**
BEACH FACES **West**

Amlwch

Valley

The rocky islets of Ynys y Fydlyn shelter a small shingle beach known as Traeth y Fydlyn (pronounced 'Try thur-vudlin'). Set in a secluded valley at the top north-west corner of Anglesey, it has good views towards the Skerries to the north and Holyhead to the south. The islets are accessible on all but the highest of tides.

Parking is as for Porth y Nant (see previous beach), and from here a public footpath leads for three quarters of a mile across sheep pastures to the beach.

1 Porth Padrig 2 Porth Newydd 3 Porth yr Hwch 4 Porth y Wig 5 Porth Gron 6 Porth Tywodog (east)

Carmel Head

Porth Padrig

GRID REF **SH 304927**
GPS **53.4040°N, 4.5521°W**
COUNTY **Isle of Anglesey**
BEACH FACES **North**

At the top north-west tip of Anglesey, the National Trust's Mynachdy estate includes the coast around Carmel Head. Proceeding clockwise from Traeth y Fydlyn, the accessible coves are:

» **Porth yr Hwch (SH 292921)** – to the south of Carmel Head, access to this pebbly beach is possible by scrambling down a very steep grassy bank.
» **Porth y Dyfn (SH 293929) and Porth y Wig (SH 296930)** – west of Carmel Head, these are narrow coves at the end of small gullies.
» **Porth yr Ebol (SH 300928)** – access is a short path following a stream on to the shore.
» **Porth Gron (SH 302927)** – a small cove backed by steep banks, best accessed from Porth yr Ebol.

» **Porth Padrig (SH 292921)** – access to this beach of shingle and rocks is a rough but easy path. On the western side of the bay is a mine adit, which can be explored with a torch.
» **Porth Newydd (SH 306929)** – a small shingle cove backed by grassy banks.
» **Porth Tywodog (SH315930)** – a long beach of shingle, some sand and a rocky lagoon. Access is from the coastal path which drops down to beach level.

Parking is at a small area just off the road at grid ref: SH 317926 (GPS: 53.4039°N, 4.5327°W), and from here a footpath follows a stream to Hen Borth. Beaches east of Carmel Head can be reached by following the coastal path westwards, but the beaches lying west and south of Carmel Head are best approached from Traeth y Fydlyn.

Note that the coastal path between Traeth y Fydlyn and Hen Borth is closed from 15 September to 31 January each year, and a diversion is in place through Mynachdy farm.

Hen Borth

GRID REF **SH 319931**
GPS **53.4076°N, 4.5292°W**
COUNTY **Isle of Anglesey**
BEACH FACES **North-west**

Hen Borth is a beach of sand and shingle backed by boulder clay, with agricultural land behind. It looks out towards the Skerries and its lighthouse, and the island of West Mouse, which has a white tower.

A very narrow lane leads to a small parking area at grid ref: SH 317926 (GPS: 53.4039°N, 4.5327°W), and from here a narrow kissing gate opens on to a footpath, following a small stream across pasture land to the beach.

The photo on the right was taken at low tide on a hot July afternoon.

Cemlyn Bay

GRID REF **SH 336932**
GPS **53.4090°N, 4.5037°W**
COUNTY **Isle of Anglesey**
BEACH FACES **North**

Owned by the National Trust, Cemlyn Bay is a crescent-shaped beach approximately 650 metres wide on Anglesey's north-west coast, between the headlands of Cerig Brith and Trwyn Cemlyn. A shingle ridge blocks off a lagoon of brackish water, which is an important breeding area for seabirds, including the common, Arctic, roseate and sandwich terns, as well as plovers and sandpipers.

Some sandy areas can be found towards the western end of the bay. Free car parking areas are situated at both ends, at grid refs: SH 336931 (GPS: 53.4089°N, 4.5043°W) and SH 329935 (GPS: 53.4120°N, 4.5157°W).

Porth y Felin & Porth y Pistyll

Porth y Felin

GRID REF **SH 343934**
GPS **53.4110°N, 4.4933°W**
COUNTY **Isle of Anglesey**
BEACH FACES **North**

Porth y Felin and Porth y Pistyll are two small shingle beaches on Anglesey's north coast, just west of Wylfa Nuclear Power Station.

To get there, from the nearby lane at grid ref: SH 348931 (GPS: 53.4094°N, 4.4858°W) a footpath leads to the coastal path. Turn right here on to a grassy track, passing some ruins on the left. As this track approaches the shore, a kissing gate (which may be partly obstructed by gorse bushes) can be seen on the left. This leads directly on to Porth y Pistyll. Porth y Felin is 350 metres west.

Porth yr Ogof & Porth Wylfa

Porth yr Ogof

GRID REF **SH 356942**
GPS **53.4186°N, 4.4741°W**
COUNTY **Isle of Anglesey**
BEACH FACES **East**

Porth yr Ogof is a tranquil cove of shingle and some sand just north of Wylfa Nuclear Power Station. On its northern side lies the small tidal island of Ynys yr Wyn and the concrete remains

of a slipway from a former lifeboat station.

Porth Wylfa lies 650 metres to the east, and is a beach of shingle backed by boulder clay banks. As with most Anglesey beaches, the shore has a good variety of pebbles.

A small, free car park with an information board, picnic table and cycle stands is located at grid ref: SH 356938 (GPS: 53.4159°N, 4.4750°W), and can be reached via a road from Tregele. A public footpath leads from the car park entrance into a wooded area where it divides: the path to the left leading to Porth yr Ogof and the one to the right leading to Porth Wylfa.

Cemaes Bay (Traeth Mawr)

GRID REF **SH 372938**
GPS **53.4155°N, 4.4499°W**
COUNTY **Isle of Anglesey**
BEACH FACES **North-west**

Cemaes has a small harbour at the mouth of the River Wygyr. The main beach, Traeth Mawr, is east of the harbour, and the smaller Traeth Bach is to the north-west. Both beaches are sandy

with some rocks and rock pools.

The harbour car park is attended, but another car park is located at the eastern side of Traeth Mawr, and some roadside parking is also available. Beach facilities include seasonal toilets and drinking water, while cafes and pubs can be found in the village. Dog restrictions apply from 1 May until 30 September on Traeth Mawr, but dogs are allowed on Traeth Bach. A beach warden is in attendance during the summer.

Porth Padrig (White Lady Bay)

GRID REF **SH 375944**
GPS **53.4210°N, 4.4457°W**
COUNTY **Isle of Anglesey**
BEACH FACES **West**

From the village of Llanbadrig a narrow lane leads to a small, free parking area next to St Patrick's church on the clifftop. Access to Porth Padrig beach is then a walk of about 300 metres back down the lane and along a short public footpath. Facing the sea, to the left of the access path, is an iron ore adit of about thirty metres, which can be explored with the aid of a torch.

The shore is sand and some rocks, with the quartzite sea stack known as the 'White Lady' in the centre of the bay. The 'White Lady' is named after Ladi Wen, a figure from Celtic mythology whose ghost is reputed to haunt Ogmore Castle in South Wales.

The car park has a stone picnic table, information board and cycle parking. An ornate kissing gate opens to the National Trust's Llanbadrig property on the headland adjacent to the church, and a stone stile at the rear of the churchyard leads to St Patrick's cave, where the saint allegedly sheltered after being shipwrecked on Middle Mouse Island.

2 Porth Cynfor **3** Porth Llanlleiana **4** Porth Llanlleiana, looking towards Middle Mouse

Porth Llanlleiana & Porth Cynfor

Porth Llanlleiana

GRID REF **SH 387951**
GPS **53.4277°N, 4.4280°W**
COUNTY **Isle of Anglesey**
BEACH FACES **North-west**

Porth Cynfor

GRID REF **SH 393949**
GPS **53.4261°N, 4.4189°W**
COUNTY **Isle of Anglesey**
BEACH FACES **North-east**

Amlwch

Valley

Llangefni

Porth Llanlleiana and Porth Cynfor are two small coves near the village of Llanbadrig. The nearby lane is very narrow and parking is difficult, but spaces can be found so long as you park responsibly and are prepared to walk. Alternatively, park as for Llanbadrig and take the coastal path.

A public footpath leads from the lane at grid ref: SH 387944 (GPS: 53.4222°N, 4.4288°W) to a track, which then continues across the bottom of the valley to a junction. Turning left here leads to Porth Llanlleiana, a narrow, rocky cove set in a steep-sided valley and backed by a derelict porcelain works (and a few picnic tables). Turning right at the junction leads to Porth Cynfor, or Hell's Mouth, a narrow cove of pebbles and some low-tide sand.

Porth Wen

GRID REF **SH 404943**
GPS **53.4215°N, 4.4029°W**
COUNTY **Isle of Anglesey**
BEACH FACES **North**

Porth Wen is a beach of shingle, low-tide rocks and rock pools, backed by steep bracken-covered banks. On the western side is a derelict brick works and a small harbour from where the bricks were exported. Access to the shore is a steep path down the bank, which is likely to be extremely slippery in wet conditions.

Parking space for two or three vehicles can be found on the sloping verge at grid ref: SH 398942 (GPS: 53.4213°N, 4.4117°W), and a public footpath (the one on the right) leads to the coastal path behind the beach. Additional parking is available on lay-bys near the junction with the A5025.

Bull Bay (Porth Llechog)

GRID REF **SH 426943**
GPS **53.4217°N, 4.3690°W**
COUNTY **Isle of Anglesey**
BEACH FACES **East**

Bull Bay is a small rocky cove near Amlwch, on Anglesey's north coast. Some roadside parking is available behind the beach, and a further small car park with toilets is situated about ninety metres back. Access to the shore, which looks out to the island of East Mouse, is down a slipway.

Porth Dynion

GRID REF **SH 436935**
GPS **53.4152°N, 4.3536°W**
COUNTY **Isle of Anglesey**
BEACH FACES **North-west**

Just west of the village of Amlwch is the tiny cove of Porth Dynion. Between low and mid tide a narrow strip of sand is exposed, with a walkway along the rocks above. A small parking area with extensive sea views is located on the clifftop, at grid ref: SH 435933 (GPS: 53.4133°N, 4.3557°W), and can be reached along a no through road signposted with a 'P' sign from the A5025. From the car park, a path to the east leads to the coastal path, from where a flight of concrete steps descends to the shore.

295

1 Porth Eilian, calm sea   **2** Porth y Corwgl   **3** Porthygwichiaid   **4** Porth Helygen

Porth Eilian & Porth y Corwgl

Porth Eilian

GRID REF **SH 476930**

GPS **53.4117°W, 4.2936°W**

COUNTY **Isle of Anglesey**

BEACH FACES **North**

Porth Eilian is a small inlet of sand and shingle near the village of Llaneilian on Anglesey's north coast. Its sheltered location makes it a good choice for sunbathing and swimming,

and sailing, scuba diving and kayaking are also popular. The lane from the village ends in a turning circle, allowing passengers to be dropped off, and access to the shore is down a slipway. A free car park and toilets are located a short walk back up the lane.

A short walk eastwards along the coastal path from Porth Eilian will lead to the tiny cove of Porth y Corwgl. There is no path down to the shore and this beach is not accessible on foot. However, the rocks just outside are easy to reach, and on a calm day it's an easy fifty-metre swim.

Porthygwichiaid

GRID REF **SH 488914**

GPS **53.3974°N, 4.2743°W**

COUNTY **Isle of Anglesey**

BEACH FACES **East**

Located on Anglesey's east coast, Porthygwichiaid, or 'Periwinkle Cove', is a secluded shingle beach approximately 350 metres wide at low tide. A public footpath leads from the nearby, very narrow lane to the coastal path. Final access to the shore is along a little-used public footpath with steep zigzag steps, which descend to the beach's northern end.

Porth Helygen & Porth yr Aber

Porth Helygen

GRID REF **SH 491908**

GPS **53.3921°N, 4.2695°W**

COUNTY **Isle of Anglesey**

BEACH FACES **East**

found at grid ref: SH 480907 (GPS: 53.3911°N, 4.2869°W) – to the coastal path, and from here a short but rugged path descends to the shore.

Half a mile to the south, the coastal path takes an inland diversion at Porth yr Aber, which is a completely rocky beach with no obvious path on to the shore.

The names 'Porth Helygen' and 'Porth yr Aber' translate as 'Willow Cove' and 'Estuary Cove' respectively.

Porth Helygen is a cove of shingle 350 metres south of Porthygwichiaid. A public footpath leads directly from the nearby narrow lane –

Portobello & Traeth Dulas

Traeth Dulas

GRID REF **SH 486889**
GPS **53.3749°N, 4.2761°W**
COUNTY **Isle of Anglesey**
BEACH FACES **East**

Traeth Dulas is the wide sand and mud estuary of the Afon Goch. At its seaward end is a small beach, backed by sandy banks covered in marram grass. The headland to the south is Craig y Sais, and at low tide it's possible to walk around to Traeth yr Ora, passing the tiny cove of Traeth Bach on the way. Ynys Dulas, an island with a tower built as a refuge for shipwrecked sailors, lies about a mile offshore.

On the north side of the river, the estate of

Portobello backs a small, sandy beach. There is no car parking nearby, but the more westerly of the two car parks for Traeth Lligwy is just over a mile away. From here, take the coastal path towards Traeth yr Ora, but instead of descending to the beach continue to an Open Access area. Then bear left towards a stile on the field boundary, which leads down to the mudflats, and turn right here to the shore.

Alternatively, parking spaces can be found at the end of the lane from Llaneuddog, at grid ref: SH 477880 (GPS: 53.3681°N, 4.2909°W); a walk of about a mile along the north side of the estuary leads to Portobello. If the tide is high, this may require a little wading. At low tide it's usually possible to wade across the river between the two beaches.

Traeth yr Ora

GRID REF **SH 489887**
GPS **53.3732°N, 4.2715°W**
COUNTY **Isle of Anglesey**
BEACH FACES **North-east**

Traeth yr Ora is undoubtedly one of Wales's best beaches. Consisting of coarse sand and shingle, it is backed by bracken-covered banks and looks out toward the island of Ynys Dulas. The name 'Traeth yr Ora' translates as 'Golden Beach'.

The nearest parking is at Traeth Lligwy, about a mile away, so the beach is usually very quiet.

Porth y Mor

GRID REF **SH 493880**
GPS **53.3670°N, 4.2652°W**
COUNTY **Isle of Anglesey**
BEACH FACES **East**

Porth y Mor, also known as Traeth Penrhyn, is a small beach of coarse sand and shingle roughly midway between Traeth yr Ora and Traeth Lligwy. Access is from the coastal path which runs along the back of the beach.

1 Traeth Lligwy, the north-western end   **2** Porth Forllwyd   **3** Traeth Lligwy

Traeth Lligwy & Porth Forllwyd

Traeth Lligwy

GRID REF **SH 497873**
GPS **53.3609°N, 4.2589°W**
COUNTY **Isle of Anglesey**
BEACH FACES **North-east**

🅿 ☕ 🌊 Ⓦⓒ

Porth Forllwyd

GRID REF **SH 503872**
GPS **53.3601°N, 4.2498°W**
COUNTY **Isle of Anglesey**
BEACH FACES **North-east**

Three quarters of a mile wide, the sandy beach of Traeth Lligwy is backed by low dunes, with low cliffs of limestone and conglomerate to the southern side. There are two car parks, both with charges; the more westerly of the two is more likely to have space during busy periods, and can be found at grid ref: SH 492873 (GPS: 53.3612°N, 4.2663°W).

Beach facilities include a cafe, toilets, drinking water, cycle stands and a picnic table. This is a popular beach for most watersports.

The bay is bounded to the south by the headland of Trwyn Gribin, and on the other side of this is the small cove of Porth Forllwyd. A small sand and shingle cove with a short harbour wall to one side, it's backed by private land and the only way to reach it is along the rocky shore from Traeth Lligwy at low tide.

Porth Helaeth & Porth yr Ynys

Porth Helaeth

GRID REF **SH 511868**
GPS **53.3568°N, 4.2376°W**
COUNTY **Isle of Anglesey**
BEACH FACES **North**

The beach at Porth Helaeth is of rocks and pebbles, backed by cliffs and bracken-covered banks. Access is from the coastal path which drops down to beach level. On the hill to the west is a memorial to the *Royal Charter* – a steam clipper on its way from Australia to Liverpool, wrecked on the rocks during the Great Storm of October 1859 with considerable loss of life.

Sometimes known Moelfre North Beach, the small shingle cove of Porth yr Ynys looks out towards the island of Ynys Moelfre, just ninety metres offshore. Access is from the coastal path which runs along the back of the beach.

Moelfre & Porth yr Aber

Moelfre

GRID REF **SH 513863**
GPS **53.3523°N, 4.2344°W**
COUNTY **Isle of Anglesey**
BEACH FACES **South-east**

The village of Moelfre on Anglesey's east coast has a beach of rocks and shingle, and looks out along the North Wales coast towards the Great Orme. Overlooking the shore is a small pay & display car park, which has plenty of seating and a snack bar. A free car park with seasonal toilets is just a short walk away in the village. Access to the shore is down a slipway.

The shingle cove of Porth yr Aber lies about 350 metres to the south and has easy access from the coastal path which drops down to near beach level.

Traeth Bychan

GRID REF **SH 515846**
GPS **53.3371°N, 4.2306°W**
COUNTY **Isle of Anglesey**
BEACH FACES **North-east**

Home to the Red Wharf Bay Sailing & Watersports Club, Traeth Bychan is a popular beach for watersports, including jet skiing and windsurfing. At high tide the beach divides into two sandy beaches to the north and south.

Access from either side is down slipways. A pay & display car park lies on the north side, and has seasonal toilets. Alternative parking can be found on the A5025 at grid ref: SH 513841 (GPS: 53.3333°N, 4.2342°W), and from here public footpaths can be followed for half a mile along either of two lanes to the beach's southern end. A beach shop/cafe is nearby, and a beach warden is in attendance during the summer.

Borth-wen & Huslan Cove

Borth-wen

GRID REF **SH 520839**
GPS **53.3310°N, 4.2227°W**
COUNTY **Isle of Anglesey**
BEACH FACES **East**

The cove of Borth-wen lies approximately halfway between Traeth Bychan and Benllech, and has a shore of pebbles, rocks and rock pools backed by low cliffs. Access from the coastal path is down a little-used path with very steep steps.

Huslan Cove, found at grid ref: SH 522830 (GPS: 53.3239°N, 4.2203°W), lies just north of Benllech Beach, and is a small cove of rocks, shingle and wave-cut platforms. Backed by low cliffs, access is down steps from the coastal path.

3 St David's Beach **4** Benllech, looking north **5** St David's Beach, a busy day

Benllech & St David's

Benllech

GRID REF **SH 524826**
GPS **53.3194°N, 4.2161°W**
COUNTY **Isle of Anglesey**
BEACH FACES **North-east**

Amlwch

Valley

Llangefni

Bangor

Situated on Anglesey's east coast, Benllech is one of the island's more popular beaches. Backed by a sea wall and promenade, this sandy beach shelves gently, providing generally safe conditions for bathing.

To the south-east the sand continues

to St David's Beach, while to the north the shore becomes rocky. A disused pipeline runs down the beach, and dog restrictions apply between it and a line of rocks to the southern end between 1 May and 30 September. Beach wardens are in attendance during the summer. Parking is at a pay & display car park, with some short-term roadside parking also available along the seafront. Facilities include a slipway, seasonal toilets, a beach shop, a cafe and a seating area with picnic tables.

St David's is a sandy beach backed by a holiday park, and the only parking available is for park residents.

Red Wharf Bay & Pentraeth Beach

Red Wharf Bay

GRID REF **SH 532810**
GPS **53.3052°N, 4.2034°W**
COUNTY **Isle of Anglesey**
BEACH FACES **East**

The hamlet of Red Wharf Bay lies on the north side of the bay it shares its name with, and has a promenade, seasonal toilets, pubs, a cafe and a small free car park. The Afon Nodwydd flows along the western side of the vast sandy beach, which is about one and a half miles square.

The opposite (south-eastern) side is known as Pentraeth Beach, and can be reached along a lane, Lon y Traeth, from Pentraeth village. This leads to a small, free parking area on firm sand. The shore here is backed by salt marsh and low dunes. On such a wide, sandy bay with little gradient, the incoming tide will flood the bay quickly. Make sure you're aware of the state of the tide if venturing any distance on to the sands.

Llanddona Beach

GRID REF **SH 569809**
GPS **53.3054°N, 4.1478°W**
COUNTY **Isle of Anglesey**
BEACH FACES **North**

On the eastern side of Red Wharf Bay, Llanddona is a wide, sandy beach backed by some shingle. Two lanes descend from Llanddona village; both are very narrow with hairpin bends and a steep gradient – thirty-five per cent or one in three. If you have a long vehicle or a trailer you'll need to park in the village and walk down. At the bottom, a lane runs along the back of the beach for a distance of about half a mile, and this part of the shore is subject to dog restrictions from 1 May to 30 September.

Facilities include seasonal toilets, drinking water, cycle stands, a beach shop/cafe and picnic tables. A beach warden is in attendance during the summer season. Parking is either at a free car park or on the shingle at the back of the beach. Popular activities include windsurfing, surfing and swimming.

Tan Dinas

GRID REF **SH 582820**
GPS **53.3156°N, 4.1288°W**
COUNTY **Isle of Anglesey**
BEACH FACES **North**

Lying below the old Tan Dinas quarries, this beach has a shore of limestone pebbles and small patches of sand, with considerable remnants of quarrying activity to the eastern side.

Access is from the coastal path at Tan Dinas farm; a public footpath leads down through a field to a kissing gate on the left. Yellow marker posts indicate the route through the next field, after which a steep track descends to the beach.

White Beach (Traeth Fedw Mawr)

GRID REF **SH 605820**
GPS **53.3162°N, 4.0943°W**
COUNTY **Isle of Anglesey**
BEACH FACES **North**

A narrow no through road, signposted as unsuitable for wide vehicles, leads to a small parking area at the National Trust's Fedw Fawr property, which has extensive views over the Irish Sea and Puffin Island and the Great Orme to the east.

White Beach is mostly limestone pebbles with some small patches of low-tide sand and access is down a steep path with steps. The beach is bounded on the eastern side by a narrow headland, the other side of which is a similar and even more secluded cove.

Caim

GRID REF **SH 620816**
GPS **53.3130°N, 4.0717°W**
COUNTY **Isle of Anglesey**
BEACH FACES **North**

Lying below the hamlet of Caim is a shore of limestone rocks and wave-cut platforms, but no sand. Fossils can be found here – particularly

corals and brachiopods – but as it's an SSSI, extracting these from the living rock is not permitted.

Access is from the west side of Caim, where a public footpath ends with a drop of about five metres to the shore, where large quarried blocks protect an area of boulder clay from erosion. This last section can be tricky, but a way down can usually be found if you look and proceed carefully.

Black Point (Trwyn Du)

GRID REF **SH 639814**
GPS **53.3117°N, 4.0431°W**
COUNTY **Isle of Anglesey**
BEACH FACES **North**

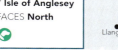

Trwyn Du, or Black Point, is at the extreme south-eastern tip of Anglesey. The beach

is rocky with some small patches of sand, backed by a storm bank of limestone pebbles. Looking out towards Puffin Island, which lies 200 metres offshore, a lighthouse stands on the intermediate low-tide rocks.

The parking area is just behind the beach on grass, and is reached via a toll road from Penmon Priory, and admission to the priory can also be gained from this toll. There is a small cafe here but no other facilities.

Penmon Beach & Lleiniog Beach

Penmon Beach

GRID REF **SH 629802**
GPS **53.3007°N, 4.0575°W**
COUNTY **Isle of Anglesey**
BEACH FACES **East**

....

Lleiniog Beach

GRID REF **SH 623793**
GPS **53.2924°N, 4.0662°W**
COUNTY **Isle of Anglesey**
BEACH FACES **East**

Amlwch

Llangefni

Bangor

Lleiniog Beach rests at the top north-eastern corner of Anglesey, about two and a half miles north of Beaumaris, and has some impressive views across the Menai Strait towards the mountains of Snowdonia and Great Orme Head. The upper shore is coarse sand and shingle, becoming muddy lower down.
A small car park with seating and picnic tables overlooks the Strait.

Penmon is the next beach to the north-east, and is a similar beach of shingle, sand and low-tide mud. Parking is in lay-bys at the southern end. Places worth visiting and within easy walking distance are Penmon Priory and St Seiriol's Well at the northern end, and the recently restored Aberlleiniog Castle a short distance back along the road to Beaumaris.

Friars Bay

GRID REF **SH 610774**
GPS **53.2750°N, 4.0848°W**
COUNTY **Isle of Anglesey**
BEACH FACES **East**

Friars Bay is a beach of coarse sand and shingle backed by a low sea wall and the B5109 from Beaumaris. It faces on to the Menai Strait, and has good views towards Snowdonia. A long lay-by on the opposite side of the road provides parking, and access is down a slipway, or by stepping over the wall.

Beaumaris Beach

GRID REF **SH 607759**
GPS **53.2615°N, 4.0887°W**
COUNTY **Isle of Anglesey**
BEACH FACES **South**

Beaumaris is better known for its castle rather than its beach, which is a mix of coarse sand and shingle extending for a short distance either side of the pier. Parking is on grass overlooking the Menai Strait, with an automatic barrier for entry.

Facilities and nearby attractions include a children's paddling pool and play area, fishing trips, cafes and bars, coin-operated toilets and the castle. Dog restrictions apply west of the pier from May to September inclusive.

Combining the counties of Denbighshire, Conwy and Flintshire, the northern coast of Wales is largely built up with a string of resort towns. The beaches tend to be long, sandy and relatively featureless, with little shelter from any wind. The main A55 and railway line to Holyhead run close to the beaches along the coastal fringe, providing easy access. For those looking to get out on two wheels, the North Wales Coastal Cycleway runs from Talacre to Penmaenmawr, and is mostly off-road and along promenades.

The largest town in this area is Llandudno, set in a bay between two limestone headlands. Rhyl and Prestatyn are further east and are the only beaches in the northern half of Wales to provide a lifeguard service. The last beach in Wales is Talacre, and further east the estuary of the Dee marks the border with Cheshire. The mountains of Snowdonia are a short distance inland – ideal for a day's walking if it's not beach weather.

THE NORTHERN COAST

Lavan Sands (Traeth Lafan)

GRID REF **SH 642730**
GPS **53.2363°N, 4.0350°W**
COUNTY **Gwynedd**
BEACH FACES **North**

Lavan Sands is a vast tidal bank of sand and mud, roughly triangular in shape, between Bangor and Llanfairfechan. A small car park is located at the Morfa Aber Nature Reserve, just north of Abergwyngregyn. The immediate shore is muddy, but a walk of half a mile in either direction leads to a narrow shoreline of light shingle, coarse sand and many cockle shells, backed by the coastal path and agricultural land.

Llanfairfechan

GRID REF **SH 678754**
GPS **53.2588°N, 3.9821°W**
COUNTY **Conwy**
BEACH FACES **North**

The village of Llanfairfechan lies on North Wales's coast, about six and a half miles east of Bangor. Its wide, sandy beach is backed by some shingle, a sea wall and promenade, and access is down slipways or steps. A free car park overlooks the shore, and can be reached by turning on to Station Road at the traffic lights in the centre of the village. Facilities include paid toilets, drinking water, a cafe, tennis courts, cycle parking, a children's paddling pool and a railway station about 200 metres from the beach. Dog restrictions apply between the two slipways from May to September inclusive.

The Afon Ddu is immediately west of the car park, and beyond it the shore becomes sandier. At low tide, the vast Lavan Sands to the west are revealed – a dangerous place to be on a rising tide. Signs warn of deep mud at low tide. The beach looks out towards Puffin Island on Anglesey, and Llandudno's Great Orme to the east.

3 Penmaenmawr **4** Penmaenmawr, with Anglesey in the distance

Penmaenmawr

GRID REF **SH 716767**
GPS **53.2714°N, 3.9256°W**
COUNTY **Conwy**
BEACH FACES **North**

Penmaenmawr is a small village on North Wales's coast, about nine miles east of Bangor. To the west of the village, the lofty granite headland of Penmaenmawr has seen plenty of quarrying activity.

The beach is sandy at low to mid tide, backed by shingle which consists of shale, grits and purple slates, as well as granite which has found its way there from the quarries.

The beach is backed by a recently refurbished promenade and a free car park, both of which run most of the length of the beach. However, the A55 dual carriageway runs just a few metres behind, so there is constant noise from the traffic. Facilities include a cafe, children's paddling pool, toilets (with a fee), seasonal first aid, drinking water, a skate park and a railway station, which lies about 200 metres from beach. Dog restrictions apply from the east side of the cafe to the sailing club slipway from 1 May to 30 September.

1 Conwy Morfa, view towards the Great Orme   **2** Conwy Morfa, looking towards Penmaen-bach Point   **3** Deganwy

Conwy Morfa Beach

GRID REF **SH 761790**
GPS **53.2931°N, 3.8591°W**
COUNTY **Conwy**
BEACH FACES **North-west**

To the west of the Afon Conwy lies Conwy Morfa – a wide, sandy and often windswept beach backed by some shingle and low dunes. Behind these are a golf course and the Morfa Conwy SSSI. Beware of the extensive sandbanks revealed at low tide, which can trap the unwary.

The main car park, which fills quickly at peak times, is reached by turning off the A55 at the Conwy junction towards the sea, then left towards the holiday park at grid ref: SH 761786 (GPS: 53.2905°N, 3.8585°W). Further parking is available at the marina, at grid ref: SH 773791 (GPS: 53.2946°N, 3.8425°W).

Deganwy

GRID REF **SH 776793**
GPS **53.2962°N, 3.8367°W**
COUNTY **Conwy**
BEACH FACES **West**

Deganwy's sandy beach borders the Conwy estuary, and is backed by shingle and a short promenade. This is no beach for paddling though: there are strong currents and swimming is not advisable. Extensive sandbanks are revealed at low tide and signs warn against venturing out on to these, but a rescue raft is moored on the largest in case anyone becomes stranded.

Some roadside parking is available on Marine Crescent, reached by turning off the A546 at the level crossing, and a small car park is located a little further north on the west side of the A546. Deganwy Railway Station and a small parade of shops are about 200 metres away.

1 Llandudno West Shore **2** Llandudno Bay, eastern end of the bay **3** Llandudno Bay

Llandudno West Shore Beach

GRID REF **SH 768816**
GPS **53.3167°N, 3.8496°W**
COUNTY **Conwy**
BEACH FACES **West**

Llandudno's West Shore Beach is backed by shingle and a promenade, with low dunes to the south and the headland of Great Ormes Head to the north. Quieter and sandier than Llandudno's main beach, there's little shelter from the wind, and windsurfing and kitesurfing are popular activities.

At low tide extensive sandbanks are revealed, which can trap the unwary. If venturing any distance from the shore be sure you know the tide times and look out for any channels in the sand which could cut off early.

Nearby facilities include toilets (with a fee), a children's play area, exercise machines, cycle parking and a cafe. Plenty of free roadside parking is available along the front of the beach or nearby, and Llandudno's railway station is a level walk of three quarters of a mile. Dog restrictions apply on a short section of the beach between the two stone groynes, from May to September inclusive.

Llandudno Bay

GRID REF **SH 785824**
GPS **53.3247°N, 3.8245°W**
COUNTY **Conwy**
BEACH FACES **North**

Set between the limestone headlands of Little Ormes Head and Great Ormes Head, the sandy, crescent-shaped beach of Llandudno Bay is a mile and three quarters long, and backed by some shingle and a wide promenade. The seafront road is lined with Victorian and Edwardian hotels and the town has all the

facilities one would expect from a major seaside resort, including a large children's paddling pool, toilets and a railway station a third of a mile away from the beach. Pay & display parking can be found along the seafront, but Llandudno's streets are very wide and it's easy to find roadside parking further back from the beach. Dog restrictions apply on the western end of the beach – from Clarence Road to the Pier – from 1 May to 30 September.

Many visitors will make the journey up the Great Orme, which can be done by tramway, cable car or walking. Reaching heights of 207 metres, the views from the top stretch as far as the Isle of Man and Blackpool Tower.

Porth Dyniewaid (Angel Bay)

GRID REF **SH 818827**
GPS **53.3238°N, 3.7758°W**
COUNTY **Conwy**
BEACH FACES **North**

Just east of the Little Orme headland is the tiny cove of Porth Dyniewaid. The shingle shore is flanked by limestone cliffs to the west side and boulders to the east, and access is down a steep bank. The beach is often used by seals for breeding, especially between September and January, and should be avoided if any are on the shore. Roadside parking can be found in the housing estate to the south-east. The limestone headland of the Little Orme rises to 141 metres, and is a much more interesting place to visit than the beach.

Penrhyn Bay

GRID REF **SH 828816**
GPS **53.3180°N, 3.7596°W**
COUNTY **Conwy**
BEACH FACES **North**

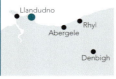

Penrhyn Bay is a wide beach of coarse sand and shingle, with stone breakwaters at either end. Backed for most of its length by a sea wall, access is down steps from the road, Glan Y Mor, and the beach's western end can be accessed by footpath from the road of Penrhyn Beach East. Roadside parking can easily be found locally.

Rhos-on-Sea

GRID REF **SH 843806**
GPS **53.3094°N, 3.7367°W**
COUNTY **Conwy**
BEACH FACES **North**

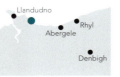

Rhos-on-Sea is at the western side of Colwyn Bay, and has a small harbour, a Tourist Information Centre, toilets and a small shopping area with cafes and bars. The shore consists of coarse sand and millions of mussel shells. Dog restrictions apply from May to September inclusive.

Colwyn Bay

GRID REF **SH 852793**
GPS **53.2979°N, 3.7227°W**
COUNTY **Conwy**
BEACH FACES **North**

Colwyn Bay is one of North Wales's main coastal resorts. Its long, sandy beach is backed by a sea wall and promenade, and access is down steps or slipways. Although there are no lifeguards here it's generally a safe beach for swimming, and dog restrictions apply between

the site of the now demolished Victoria Pier and the entrance to Eirias Park from 1 May to 30 September. Roadside pay & display parking is available along most of the promenade, and local facilities include refreshment kiosks, a bouldering wall and toilets. The town centre is a five-minute walk away and has a railway station, shopping centre, cafes, banks and pubs.

Old Colwyn is to the east of Colwyn Bay, and this part of the beach only shows itself from low to mid tide. The sandy shore is backed by a promenade, and a good variety of seashells can be found. Roadside parking is available and access is down steps.

Llanddulas

GRID REF **SH 906787**
GPS **53.2936°N, 3.6415°W**
COUNTY **Conwy**
BEACH FACES **North**

Llanddulas's rocky beach hosts the remains of wooden groynes, with some sand showing around low tide. The beach is backed by North Wales Coastal Cycleway and the main railway

line to Holyhead. Just to the east, the river Dulas meanders through a grassed area before emerging on to the shore.

Two free parking areas overlook the shore, and are located just a few hundred metres from the Llanddulas junction of the A55 North Wales Expressway. Access to the shore is down a slipway and toilets are the only facilities. If you walk the quarter of a mile to Llanddulas village you'll find a wider range of facilities, including a few small shops and two pubs.

Pensarn

GRID REF **SH 946788**
GPS **53.2953°N, 3.5816°W**
COUNTY **Conwy**
BEACH FACES **North**

Pensarn's long, sandy beach is backed by a wide shingle bank, a sea wall and promenade. The free car parks are just behind the beach with some parking possible on the shingle. Facilities include toilets, cafes, cycle parking and the Abergele & Pensarn Railway Station, which is almost on the beach. The market town of Abergele is three quarters of a mile inland and has a good shopping street. Dog restrictions apply from May to September inclusive, between Queensway and a point ninety metres west of Sea Road.

Kinmel Bay

GRID REF **SH 983805**
GPS **53.3113°N, 3.5266°W**
COUNTY **Conwy**
BEACH FACES **North**

Also known as Sandy Cove Beach, Kinmel Bay is a wide beach of low-tide sand, backed by a pebble bank, sea defence walls and a promenade. Behind this are holiday parks and private residential estates, with a cyclepath running along the promenade. A popular spot for watersports such as windsurfing and kitesurfing, swimming is generally safe here, and dog restrictions apply between Dinas Avenue and Sandbank Road from May to September inclusive. A small pay & display car park can be found at the end of St Asaph Road, which leaves the A548 half a mile east of the railway bridge.

3 Rhyl, beach level   **4** Rhyl   **5** Rhyl, East Beach looking towards Prestatyn

Rhyl

GRID REF **SJ 005820**
GPS **53.3252°N, 3.4941°W**
COUNTY **Denbighshire**
BEACH FACES **North**

Rhyl's sandy Central Beach is backed by a sea wall and promenade, with the River Clwyd emerging at the western end. This can create fast and dangerous currents, and although bathing is generally safe on the main beach, at low tide it can be a half-mile walk to the sea.

Sandbanks can also be a hazard for the unwary. Lifeguards patrol from the end of May until early September and during weekends and school holidays, and Rhyl East Beach has a zone set up for windsurfing and kayaking. Dogs are not allowed on any of the beaches from May to September inclusive.

Facilities include plenty of cafes, a skate park, pitch & putt, a children's paddling pool, toilets, a Tourist Information Centre, a SeaQuarium, and a railway station approximately 650 metres from the beach. The town centre also has a good range of shops.

Prestatyn

GRID REF **SJ 042833**
GPS **53.3376°N, 3.4389°W**
COUNTY **Denbighshire**
BEACH FACES **North**

The town of Prestatyn has wide, sandy beaches which are interspersed with stone groynes and backed by a promenade and cyclepaths. Behind this are holiday camps and parkland.

The main beach, a Blue Flag beach known as Central Beach, is patrolled by lifeguards from late May until early September during weekends and school holidays. Ffrith Beach, found at grid ref: SJ 043832 (GPS: 53.3370°N, 3.4379°W), lies about a mile to the west, and has a similar shore backed by a promenade, and Barkby Beach, found at grid ref: SJ 074843 (GPS: 53.3483°N, 3.3922°W), lies to the east. Here the promenade ends and sand dunes take over. Watersports are popular, and in summer a buoyed channel is in place on Barkby Beach for the launching of jet skis and powercraft.

Parking is at pay & display car parks overlooking the shore, and facilities include cafes, toilets, a leisure centre, an adventure playground and beach shops. Prestatyn Railway Station is approximately half a mile from Central Beach. Although dog restrictions apply from May to September, dogs are allowed on the west end of Ffrith Beach and to the east of Barkby Beach where the promenade ends.

4 Talacre, looking east **5** Talacre **6** Talacre, the car park

Talacre

GRID REF **SJ 121851**
GPS **53.3551°N, 3.3208°W**
COUNTY **Flintshire**
BEACH FACES **North**

Located at the most northerly point of mainland Wales, Talacre (pronounced 'Ta-lakree') is a wide, sandy and often windswept beach which provides a relief from the more commercialised resorts of the North Wales Coast. The disused Point of Ayr lighthouse (reputedly haunted by the ghost of a former keeper) stands in the centre of the beach. Strong currents render the sea unsuitable for swimming and most other watersports.

Behind the beach is the Gronant Dunes SSSI, which is home to the rare sand lizard and natterjack toad. Local facilities include toilets, a cafe, a pub, shops and a post office. Free car parking on rough sandy ground is available just behind the dunes, at the very end of the road.

Wales has numerous offshore islands, but few have any beaches to speak of. Those which do – Flat Holm, Caldey Island, Ramsey Island and Bardsey Island – are listed in the following pages. Spanning the length of Wales, all of these islands are owned by organisations, and though access is not allowed on some, there are still some hidden gems to be found.

THE
ISLANDS

Opposite St Margaret's Island, the causeway from Caldey Island

Flat Holm

Coal Beach

GRID REF **ST 222651**
GPS **51.3791°N, 3.1180°W**
COUNTY **Vale of Glamorgan**
BEACH FACES **North-east**

Situated in the murky waters of the Bristol Channel about two and a half miles off the coast of South Wales, the island of Flat Holm is the southernmost point in Wales. Famous for the first ever transmission of radio signals over the sea by Guglielmo Marconi in 1897, it is now managed by Cardiff Council as a Nature Reserve and SSSI, and has resident wardens all year round. Boat trips run from Cardiff Bay in summer and

unofficial landings are also permitted, but all visitors must pay a landing fee. Facilities include toilets and a tiny pub, The Gull and Leek, with outdoor seating. Buildings include a lighthouse, a derelict isolation hospital, numerous World War Two lookouts and gun emplacements. Dogs are not allowed.

Coal Beach and neighbouring East Beach are the arrival points for boats from the mainland, situated on the north-east corner. Both consist of steeply sloping shingle, mostly mudstone, limestone and some flint, and access is down good paths with steps.

On the north-west corner lies West Beach. Also consisting of rocks and shingle, it's probably the island's best beach. On very low tides it's possible to walk around the island along the shore, and the two small coves of Point Bay and Dripping Cove become accessible.

Caldey Island

Priory Bay

GRID REF **SS 137970**
GPS **51.6404°N, 4.6927°W**
COUNTY **Pembrokeshire**
BEACH FACES **North-west**

H'west   ● Narberth

Tenby

Caldey Island lies about two thirds of a mile off the Pembrokeshire coast at its closest point. Priory Bay is the largest beach on the island and the arrival point for the boats from Tenby – the departure point being Tenby's Castle Beach (see page 78). The crossing takes about twenty-five minutes and the service operates Monday to Friday from Easter until October, and on Saturdays from May to September. The island is privately owned by Cistercian monks, and

unofficial landings are not permitted. Caldey village is just a short walk away, and has toilets, a cafe with outdoor seating, a post office and a gift shop. Dogs are allowed on the island but must be kept on a lead.

Priory Bay beach is made up of coarse sand with some pebbles, backed by low dunes, and is generally safe for bathing. West of Priory Bay the shore becomes rocky, but at low tide it's possible to walk past Eel Point to Sandy Bay – a small beach of steeply sloping sand and some pebbles, backed by limestone cliffs and several small caves. To the west of Caldey, St Margaret's Island is separated by the channel of Little Sound at high tide and a causeway at low tide.

Continuing anticlockwise around Caldey, the next beach is Sandtop Bay on the island's west side. The coastal path has recently been extended to this side of the island, but there

is no official public access to the beach. Swimming is dangerous due to its proximity to the strong currents of Little Sound.

The only beach on Caldey's southern coast is the inaccessible Red Berry Bay. The small, sandy bay of Drinkim on the eastern coast is one of the island's better beaches and is backed by a small pebble bank and high cliffs.

Swimming is dangerous due to strong currents just offshore. There is no official public access, and the only way on to the shore is a scramble down a steep path with fixed ropes alongside. A little further north, the picturesque sandy cove of Bullum's Bay is flanked by low limestone cliffs and backed by fields.

3 Porth Lleuog **4** Abermawr **5** Abermawr and Cadair Rhwydog

Ramsey Island

Abermawr

GRID REF: **SM 700243**
GPS: **51.8693°N, 5.3413°W**
COUNTY **Pembrokeshire**
BEACH FACES **West**

St Davids

H'west

Owned by the RSPB, Ramsey Island is separated from mainland Pembrokeshire by the half-mile-wide tidal race of Ramsey Sound. Open daily from 10 a.m. to 4 p.m. between 1 April and 31 October, boats run from St Justinian's with a crossing time of about ten minutes.

Abermawr on the west coast is the island's largest beach – a bay of sand and shingle surrounded by cliffs of mudstone and tuff. A steep path descends to the shore, but public access is not allowed.

South of Abermawr is Cader Rhwydog, the highest point on the island at 136 metres. On the other side of this is Porth Lleuog, a narrow cove of shingle and some low-tide sand. Although easily accessible by a steep path down a gully, this too is off limits to the public. Refreshments and toilets are available, but dogs are not allowed on the island.

Bardsey Island

Porth Solfach

GRID REF: **SH 113213**
GPS: **52.7559°N, 4.7966°W**
COUNTY **Gwynedd**
BEACH FACES **West**

Lying about two miles offshore from the Llŷn Peninsula across the notorious tidal race of Bardsey Sound, Bardsey Island is approximately a mile long and half a mile wide. At 167 metres, its highest point is Mynydd Enlli. It has two beaches about a hundred metres apart on either side of a narrow isthmus.

Porth Solfach on the west side is the better of the two, and is a small bay of steeply sloping white sand and shingle, backed by low boulder clay banks. The lower shore consists of seaweed-covered rocks and rotting seaweed.

Henllwyn West faces east and is mostly shingle with small patches of sand, and some seaweed-covered rocks. A small quay at its northern end is the arrival point for boat trips from the mainland. Refreshments and toilets are available, but dogs are not allowed on the island.

Glossary

Bight A wide bay formed by a concave shoreline, or the sea area between two headlands.

Bill A narrow promontory.

Causeway A tidal road or other crossing, usually between an island and the mainland.

Chart datum Often seen on Tide Tables. A level from which water depths and tide heights are measured. Usually the lowest possible calculated tide height, so that tide tables will never show a negative height.

Doline A depression in the ground caused by the collapse of a limestone cave.

Dumping waves Waves where the wave face develops a concave shape, causing the crest to drop – usually with force – on to the shore.

Dune slack The low-lying areas of sand dunes, where vegetation usually flourishes.

Ebb tide A falling tide – the 'drop' in surfing terms.

Estuary The tidal section of a river.

Fathom Unit of water depth equal to six feet.

Flood tide A rising tide – the 'push' in surfing terms.

Foreshore The area of the beach between high and low tide.

Groyne A stone or timber barrier on the beach, to reduce erosion and longshore drift.

Isthmus A narrow strip of land through water, connecting two larger land areas.

Lagoon An area of seawater, separated at low tide from the sea by rocks, reefs or sand.

Land breeze A light wind blowing from land to sea, caused by a temperature differential. Usually occurring after a hot day.

Living rock Rock which is still part of the earth, such as the cliffs or bedrock.

Localism Preference for one's own area. In the context of this book, a dislike of people who aren't local – particularly by surfers.

Longshore drift The movement of material along the coast by waves and tidal currents.

Marsh An area of wet or muddy low-lying ground, frequently flooded by the sea or rivers.

Neap tides Tides which occur around the time of a quarter moon. These have the lowest tidal range.

Offshore wind Winds blowing from the land to the sea.

Onshore wind Winds blowing from the sea to the land.

Perigean spring tide An exceptionally high, and low, spring tide which occurs when the moon's orbit brings it closest to Earth.

Promontory High land that protrudes out into the sea.

Purl (verb) To flow with a soft rippling sound, such as streams across a beach.

Race A strong tidal current flowing through a narrow channel, such as between the mainland and Ramsey or Bardsey Island.

Reef Rocks or sand just below the surface of the sea.

Reef break (Surfing) The point of a reef which waves break over.

Ria A narrow inlet of a river valley, open to the sea.

Rip current A strong current flowing out to sea.

Road A sheltered area of water where boats can lie safely at anchor.

Salt marsh A marshy, muddy area often flooded by the sea, usually near river estuaries.

Sandbar/Sandbank A bank of sand projecting out into the sea, and a dangerous place to be on an incoming tide.

Sea breeze A light wind blowing in from the sea, caused by a temperature differential. Usually occurs on hot days.

Sea mist Moisture-laden air being carried in on a sea breeze.

Storm bank A steep pebble bank at the back of the beach formed by storm tides.

The Beaches: at a glance

Popular beaches with plenty of facilities nearby

Anglesey
Benllech 303
Newborough Beach 249
Rhosneigr Beach 258
Trearddur Bay 265

Carmarthenshire
Pembrey Beach 59

Ceredigion
Aberystwyth North 175
Borth 178
New Quay Harbour 165

The Llŷn Peninsula
Abersoch 212
Criccieth 204

Meirionnydd
Aberdyfi 182
Barmouth 188
Tywyn 184

The Northern Coast
Colwyn Bay 320
Llandudno Bay 317
Llandudno West Shore Beach 317
Llanfairfechan 312
Prestatyn 324
Rhyl 323

Pembrokeshire
Saundersfoot 73
Tenby Castle Beach 78
Tenby North 77
Tenby Harbour 77

South-East Wales
Aberavon Sands 27
Barry Island (Whitmore Bay) 7
Sandy Bay 22
Southerndown 18

Swansea and Gower
Caswell Bay 35
Langland Bay 34
Port Eynon 42

Dog-friendly beaches

Anglesey
Aberffraw Bay 253
Porth Tywyn Mawr 277
Traeth Lligwy 300
Traeth yr Ora 298

Carmarthenshire
Burry Port Beach 58
Telpyn Beach 67

Ceredigion
Cei Bach 166
Traeth Gwyn 166
Ynyslas Estuary Beach 179

The Llŷn Peninsula
Abererch Beach 206
Hell's Mouth 215
Porthdinllaen 234
Traeth Penllech 225
The Warren 210

Meirionnydd
Cemetery Beach 183
Morfa Dyffryn 190
Shell Island 192

The Northern Coast
Conwy Morfa Beach 314
Penrhyn Bay 318
Talacre 325

Pembrokeshire
Broad Haven South 90
Caerfai Bay 123
Freshwater West 96
Marloes Sands 109
Monkstone 75
Newport Sands 144
Pwllgwaelod 140

South-East Wales
Jackson's Bay 7
Kenfig Sands 25
Margam Sands 26
Merthyr Mawr Beach 20
Newton Bay 21
Ogmore-by-Sea 19

Swansea and Gower
Jersey Marine Beach 30
Llangennith 51
Oxwich Bay 42
Three Cliffs Bay 40
Whiteford Sands 54

Lifeguarded beaches

Carmarthenshire
Pembrey Beach 59
Pendine Sands 64

Ceredigion
Aberporth 152
Aberystwyth North 175
Aberystwyth South 174
Borth 178
Clarach Bay 177
Llangrannog 157
New Quay Harbour 165
Tresaith 154

The Northern Coast
Prestatyn 324
Rhyl 323

Pembrokeshire
Amroth 70
Broad Haven 115
Freshwater West 96
Newport Sands 144
Nolton Haven 117
Newgale Sands 118
Poppit Sands 145
Saundersfoot 73
Tenby Castle Beach 78
Tenby North 77
Tenby South 78
Whitesands Bay 127

South-East Wales
Aberavon Sands 27
Barry Island (Whitmore Bay) 7
Kenfig Sands 25
Llantwit Major 12
Ogmore-by-Sea 19
Rest Bay 24
Sandy Bay 22
Southerndown 18
Trecco Bay 21

Swansea and Gower
Bracelet Bay 32
Caswell Bay 35
Langland Bay 34
Port Eynon 42
Three Cliffs Bay 40

Quiet, secret beaches or coves

Anglesey
Porth Aels *254*
Porthygwichiaid *296*
Tan Dinas *305*
Traeth Abermenai *248*
Traeth yr Ora *298*
Traeth y Fydlyn *285*

Carmarthenshire
Morfa Bychan *65*
Scott's Bay *62*
Tywyn Point *60*

Ceredigion
Traeth Bach *156*
Traeth Gwrddon *151*
Traeth Socen *162*
Traeth y Coubal *165*
Traeth-yr-ynys *158*

The Llŷn Peninsula
Carreg Wen *202*
Porth Fechan *206*
Porth Lefesig *222*
Porth Pistyll *237*
Tan y Graig *240*

Pembrokeshire
Aber Rhigian *142*
Box Bay (with difficult access) *89*
Longoar Bay *101*
Porth Dwcan (with difficult access) *134*
Porthmynawyd *120*
Presipe Bay *82*
Pwllcrochan Bay *135*
Pwllstrodur *132*
Waterwynch Bay *76*

South-East Wales
Monknash *16*
Temple Bay *17*

Swansea and Gower
Blue Pool Bay *52*
Pwlldu Bay *37*
Tor Bay *41*

Surf beaches

Anglesey
Aberffraw Bay *253*
Porth Dafarch *268*
Rhosneigr Beach *258*

Ceredigion
Aberporth *152*
Aberystwyth South *174*
Borth *178*
Llangrannog *157*
Penbryn Beach *155*

The Llŷn Peninsula
Hell's Mouth *215*
Porth Ceiriad *214*

Meirionnydd
Barmouth *188*
Tywyn *184*

Pembrokeshire
Abermawr *133*
Freshwater West *96*
Manorbier *84*
Newgale Sands *118*
Westdale Bay *108*
Whitesands Bay *127*

South-East Wales
Llantwit Major *12*
Margam Sands *26*
Rest Bay *24*
Southerndown *18*

Swansea and Gower
Broughton Bay (for the experienced only) *53*
Caswell Bay *35*
Langland Bay *34*
Llangennith *51*

Within walking distance of a railway station

Carmarthenshire
Burry Port Beach *58*
Ferryside *61*

Ceredigion
Aberystwyth North *175*
Aberystwyth South *174*
Borth *178*

The Llŷn Peninsula
Abererch Beach *206*
Criccieth *204*
Pwllheli South Beach *208*

Meirionnydd
Aberdyfi *182*
Barmouth *188*
Llandanwg *192*
Llwyngwril *186*
Tywyn *184*

The Northern Coast
Colwyn Bay *320*
Deganwy *314*
Llandudno Bay *317*
Llanfairfechan *312*
Penmaenmawr *313*
Pensarn *322*
Prestatyn *324*
Rhyl *323*

Pembrokeshire
Fishguard Beaches *138*
Penally *78*
Tenby South *78*

South-East Wales
Barry Island (Whitmore Bay) *7*
Jackson's Bay *7*
Penarth *2*
Watch House Bay *8*

Index